CAplus-3

in

✓ Windows Appreciation
✓ Internet Appreciation
✓ Threat Appreciation, and
✓ Evaluation of PC Quality

for basic and advanced learning

N. Stephen

N. Stephen

CAplus-3

Published By:
Space-Era Data Service,
www.onlineworkdata.com

Printed and Distributes By:
CreateSpace Independent
Publishing Platform,

4900 LaCross Road,
North Charleston, SC 29406, USA

First Edition

ISBN-13: 978-1506021355
ISBN-10: 1506021352

DEDICATION

This book is dedicated to God Almighty, first for the salvation He gave to me, second for His guidance and third, His provisions in my life. In addition, is to my lovely Mum, Mrs. Nwankwo Grace, a woman of a singular merit and honor, who, though young and beautiful devoted herself entirely to the rearing of my education. May the Almighty God through my Lord Jesus Christ extends her days with divine health. Amen!

THE BOOK CONTENTS

Acknowledgments--- i

Preface--- ii

General Introduction of CAplus-- iii

General Introduction of the Book--- 1

Chapter One-----   **Windows Appreciation---**.------------------------------------- 3

   ■ Topic   Setting up a Desktop Computer------------------------------ 4

      "   Windows and Desktop Introduction---------------------------

                                                                    7

      "   Exploring The Desktop Environment------------------------

                                                                    10

      "   Brief About Windows Accessories------------------------------

                                                                    23

            Introduction to Windows Control Panel----------------------

                                                                    25

            Introduction to Command Prompt Application--------------

                                                                    27

            Introducing MS Office Suits and Applications----------------

                                                                    28

            Brief of Character, Bit, Byte, Data, and Information---------

                                                                    33

            Introduction to File-naming Convention----------------------

                                                                      34

            How to Publish and Print in PDF and XPS Document-----

                                                                    40

            Key terminologies and Meanings------------------------------ 43

Chapter Two-----   **Internet Appreciation**---

                                                                  45

   ■ Topic   Actual and Virtual Activities of Internet----------------------- 47

   ■ "   Intrinsic of Internet--- 47

   ■ "   Brief About CAPTCHA--------------------------------------- 62

            Key terminologies and Meanings------------------------------ 63

Chapter Three---   **Computer Threat Appreciation---**------------------------------- 65

   ▪ Topic   What is Computer Malware------------------------------------- 66

   ▪ "   What is Computer Virus--- 68

   ▪ "   Who Creates Virus and Why?----------------------------------- 68

   ▪ "   Classifications of Virus--- 70

   ▪ "   The History of Computer Virus-------------------------------- 73

   ▪ "   The Symptoms of Computer Virus----------------------------- 74

   ▪ "   Computer Threat Prevention----------------------------------- 75

   ▪ "   How to Prevent Computer Threats---------------------------- 76

   ▪   How to Remove Computer Threats---------------------------- 82

      Key terminologies and Meanings------------------------------- 88

Chapter Four-   **Evaluation of PC Quality (EPCQ)**-------------------------- 89

   ▪ Topic   Analyzing the External Information---------------------------- 90

   ▪ "   Analyzing the Internal Information---------------------------- 93

   ▪ "   Performing Information and Tools Rating--------------------- 94

   ▪ "   EPCQ Based on Utility Software------------------------------ 97

   ▪ "   EPCQ Conclusion for Windows Computers----------------- 105

   ▪   Key terminologies and Meanings------------------------------ 106

   ▪   Practical Activities of the Book------------------------------- 107

References--- 111

Index-- 112

ACKNOWLEDGMENTS

I acknowledged with a profound gratitude the efforts of my friend, Pastor Beloved Osi, for her sense of commitment and effort in the project. She strongly participated in the grammatical and spelling check of the manuscript. Not to forget is Mr. Nnamdi. Chris, the Director of Tourch Information Technology Centre Nigeria for encouragement, and the Director of LordKel Digital Production, Mr. Kelvin Joseph and his workers for designing the front cover image of the book.

PREFACE

As most people know, the World has gone into a technological revolution. In the forefront of this revolution is an electronic machine with superlative functions, and capabilities in the application of works of lives. The impact analysis of this 'machine' shows that its available programs and services are multiplying every day, therefore all aspect of human activities ranging from learning and communication practices, marketing, information searching, research works, business transactions, social networking, medical services, and others are presently engulfed with it. So the use of the machine is at exponential increase in order to enable this present generation improved on works of lives. But, ignorance has denied many people the knowledge of this great machine, known as *'computer'*. Although, not in all countries, as the case is in some *More Developed Countries (MDCs)*,but to some regions of the World like the *Less Developed Countries (LDCs)* were the appreciation and learning is not intensive. Truly, there is a large computer-knowledge-gap between those living with the knowledge, and those who have not appreciate the knowledge, and this therefore, calling the need for computer appreciation, not only to LDCs, but also to some members of MDCs.

The term *"Computer Appreciation"* was coined by Richard W. Hamming (circa 1960) when he indicated the need for broad scale education about computers (Arthur B. Kahn, 1967)[1]. In other words, Hamming advocacy emphasized on the need to expand the learning of computer in order to improve the course of education scale, especially in countries where there is such need. So to achieve this objective, people have to begin the learning of computer in order to sharpen their future, which is partly framed in computer technology. They must in their various facets of works embrace the trend by being computer literate so that the future generation will inherit a good work done for the society.

Supportively, **CAplus (KA+)** is part of the solution. It is a written work for basic and advance learning of computer, and are in ***book-one, two, three, and four*** format. The author who has more than 16 years computing experience as of when it was written made an intensive gathering of knowledge together with his experience to write about it, within a period of 3-4 years. The **'plus'** added to the name (i.e. computer appreciation plus) indicates that the books are more than a mere computer appreciation book. The basic part of the books are written to serve as the first step for computer learning beginners, which included those at the tertiary level, pupils in secondary schools, and private individuals who are professionals in various areas of works. And the advance part is to support the computer application knowledge of the intermediate and advance computer users. The author welcomes the general public for the uses of the books.

N. Stephen
February 15 2015.

1. Arthur B. Kahn stated this in his book titled "An Appreciation of Computer Appreciation. Published in ACM New York, NY, USA, 1967.

GENERAL INTRODUCTION OF CAplus

By computer appreciation, we are referring to the technology impart of understanding computer through learning and practicing the first-step of its composition, scope, and operations in ICT World. This is for basic, but for advanced computer appreciation, it is to support the computer application knowledge of the intermediate and advance computer users, who perform their daily activities with computer.

By comparison, appreciation is different from "computer application", which is the technical impart of understanding how to use application programs of computer through practice. In other words, the key difference between both of them is that the capability attachment of the later (computer application) depends on the former (computer appreciation). Meaning that the ability to perform effectively in computer application depends on the knowledge gained from the computer appreciation. Following this point, the package of **CAplus** are to help users gain and improve in both computer appreciation and application. To achieve this point, the package is booked into **CAplus-1, 2, 3, and 4.**

For **CAplus-1**, it consists of section-one and two. The *Section-One* contains chapter one to five with the topics on history of computer, the meaning, attributes and uses of computers, including the classifications of computer, common components basic operations of computer relatively. It runs to counter the myth-belief that many people have over computer. This is because many never accept the nature of computer as not being a voodoo machine. The limitations of computer are still in doubt, and the ability to identify any machine that belongs to the families of computers is not yet clarified to some people. In addition, the last chapter emphasized on how computer carries out its common operations such as input-processing-output functions in relation to its various components.

Section-Two is titled "building computer career" theme, which comprises six examples of computer career topics, with cases of teaching students on how to build and enhance computer careers through educational system, participatory in application program training, and relative software to each specialized area of the career. For instance, a topic was taught based on the best software and guidelines that computer science career person has to undergo in order to realize the goals of the career.

The **CAplus-2** was written for advanced-level in order to help students in studying of computer's components. To support its central teaching, the book explained the hardware and software components of computer, and how they function systematically in the work process of computation. In this form, the knowledge-gained about these components will help students in learning computer maintenance and repair, troubleshooting identification, and how to manage computer threats as all of them are the central teachings in **CAplus-4**, which also taught about the basic maintenance and repair of Windows Computers.

For the **CAplus-3**, the general study of computer appreciation is not complete without the introduction of computer application, and since Windows Operating System (OS) is the main OS in the work of CAplus, therefore "windows appreciation" was written as a prepared take-off ground for computer application training. To widen the book, the concept of file, and folder were treated, including other Chapter topics on "internet appreciation", "computer threats appreciation", and "evaluating of PC quality."

Generally, it is advisable to use both **CAplus-1, 2, 3,** and **4** in order to achieve the complete benefit-effectiveness of the package.

Notes

1.   As you proceed, do not put away this book when any part of the objective is not achieved.

2.   If you have any kind of comment or question, for support, visit www.onlineworkdata.com.

Some Key Terms

*Anti-Malware
*Anti-Virus
*Bloggers
*Bots
*CAPTCHA
*Command Prompt
*Computer Threat
*Control Panel
*Desktop Actions
*Desktop Computer
*Desktop Environment
*Dialog Box
*Display Resolution Size
*Emulator
*Folder
*Icon
*IP Address
*Local Disk
*Malware
*Model
*MS Office
*Spam box
*Spammers
*Syntax Line
*System Brand
*System Tools
*Table Desktop
*Task Manager
*Tower Desktop
*Trojan
*Virus
*WEI Rating
*Windows
*Windows Accessories

✓ **Windows Appreciation**
✓ **Internet Appreciation**
✓ **Computer Threat Appreciation**
✓ **Evaluation of PC Quality**

Chapter Studies

The Chapter Studies are grouped into the followings:

1. Chapter One-Windows Appreciation
2. Chapter Two-Internet Appreciation
3. Chapter Three-Computer Threat Appreciation
4. Chapter Four-Evaluation of PC Quality

Practical Activities

There are series of practical activities at the end.

Objectives of the Studies

At the end of the study, Students should be able to:
- know how to setup a desktop computer;
- know the basic integral parts of Desktop;
- know the basic integral parts of Windows;
- know the basic, necessary, uses and functions of the control panel of Windows Operating System;
- gain the preparation ground for Windows and other software maintenance;
- know how to access the Windows tools of a computer;
- know the components of Windows Operating System;
- understand the scope of Internet and its application;
- understand what is virus and malware;
- understand how to remove and prevent computer threat;
- and, how to evaluate the quality of a personal computer.

GENERAL INTRODUCTION OF THE BOOK

By Windows Appreciation, we are referring to the learning activities in order to gain a comprehensive practical and theoretical knowledge of Windows Application for the purpose of taking advantage in Computer Application. For the other, by Computer Threat, we are referring to "the number one enemy of computer users", which is bound to exist in the computer world. It is very necessary for us to gain a requisite knowledge of computer threat, which is the enemy of our data and computer.

Briefly, Windows is the software interactive platform between a computer user and the computer. It varies between Windows of Windows OS, and Windows of Application Software. The former is the Windows environment standing as an interactive platform between a computer user and the Operating System, while the latter is the Windows of Application Software, which stands as an interactive platform between a computer user and Application Software. Nevertheless, it is not possible to discuss Windows without the appreciating of Internet. This is because working with Windows is not only an offline activity, but also an online activity, which requires Internet application, therefore placing users to know Internet appreciation and application.

An Internet is a global computer networks that connect available computers together for viewing and sharing information all over the world. With Internet facility we can communicate effectively and efficiently with people, despite their place of locations, make quick and large research, and gain access to many information. It is requisite in computer uses and learning, but as well exposes users to some risk of loss of private information to unknown persons due to malware infiltration on a computer.

Malware and virus are computer threat. They are the commonest enemy of computers. A computer threat is any program created specifically to invade into computers and networks without owner's awareness and create havoc on them by destroying the targeted areas. Some threats are mere annoying without much harmfulness, but others can do serious damage, they can delete or change files, steal important information, load and run unwanted applications, send documents via electronic mail (email), or even damage the Windows OS of computer. They can as well spy users' information and send them to their developers, and do other dangerous activities. Moreover, it is not only malware that can deny us the fun of using our computers, but when we do not have knowledge over the components made with our computer, it affects us. This is because we might mishandle the computer, thus fault it.

So how to evaluate the quality of a PC (computer) is by identifying both some internal and external information that makeup the PC. For example, understanding the RAM size of a particular computer can help us determine the kind and size of application software to install on that computer

From the above explanation, Chapter one is the place for Windows Appreciation, while Chapter two focused on Internet Appreciation, and Chapter three is for Threat Appreciation. Moreover, it is sufficient to understand the quality of computers we used, so Chapter four treated on how to evaluate the quality of a PC.

Chapter One
Windows Appreciation

INTRODUCTION

In computer's terminology, the word 'Windows' is associated with Microsoft Corporation Operating System, which is known as Microsoft Windows, and by Windows Appreciation, we are referring to the learning processes of gaining a comprehensive theoretical knowledge of Windows Application for the purpose of Computer Application. Moreover, as we learnt in the Software topic of CAplus-1 book, Windows System, although been Operating System software is also a Graphic User Interface (GUI) component constituting of desktop environment that supports window managers' implementation, and provisions of basic function support to graphic hardware like mouse, keyboard, and others. For work usage, it enables a computer user to work with several programs at the same time. In this condition, each program is designed to run on its window, which is generally a rectangular area of the screen, and most windows have basic support of re-parenting, which they overlap each other or, flip in pages with *'backward and forward'* buttons support.. But, Windows System is not the only Computer System (i.e. Operating System). There are others such as Mac, and Linux System. But, we choose Windows System because of its popularity over the others. Despite this, a user may decide to reformat a computer that came with Windows System and replace it with another Computer System, perhaps Linux or Mac OS. So considering what we learnt in CAplus-1 book, it is assumed that we have acquired the full knowledge about computer, especially in the theoretical point of view. For instance, we know what computer is about, how it works, and the components or parts that made what it is. So in this Chapter, we are working on how to access and use our computer in the need of application, by appreciating the basic Windows components that stands as physical interface of Windows Operation, therefore, we will look into the general Windows of an Application Software, and the Windows of Window OS.

SETTING UP A DESKTOP COMPUTER

When we unpacked a desktop computer, the main hardware, which are monitor, system unit, and keyboard, including mouse (which is a peripheral hardware) are set apart individually. It is only when they are connected together that we can be able to power 'on' the computer and make use of it. However, this is not like a Laptop where the whole components already have been assembled together as a package. By identification, desktop computers are classified into two main categories, which are Table Desktop, and Tower Desktop. See below pictures.

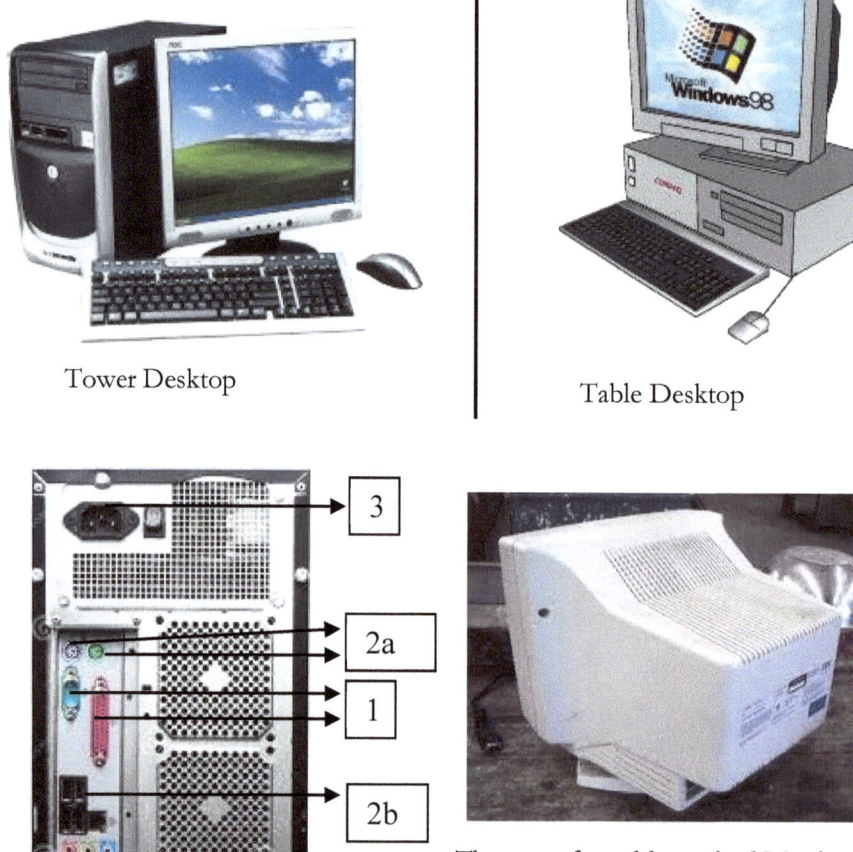

Tower Desktop

Table Desktop

The rear of a System unit

The rear of an old standard Monitor

Below is in align with the label of the System Unit:

- From the left is the VGA port, and to the right is the DVI port.

- The 2a is PS/2 port for keyboard, and while the second port is for the mouse. For the 2b, shows the USB ports.

- The label 3 is the Power supply port.

1. <u>Connecting the System Unit and Monitor with the VGA Cable:</u> The VGA (Video Graphics Array) Cable is always with a blue head. If it is not VGA, it will be DVI (Digital Video Imaging), which has a stainless head.

VGA cable or cord

DVI cable or cord

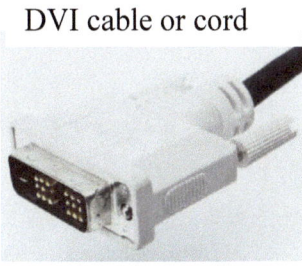

The rear is of a Table Desktop, from the left is the DVI port, and to right is the VGA port.

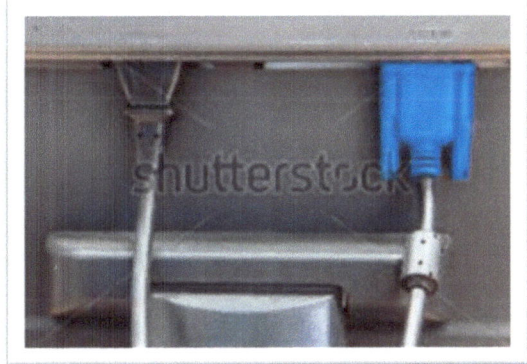

From the left is the Power Supply cable connected to its port, and to the right is the VGA cable connected to its port, all at the rear of a Monitor.

 The cable is made to fit the ports, if it fails, do not force it.

2. **Connecting the Keyboard and the Mouse on the System Unit:** The old port standard for mouse and keyboard is PS/2, but unfortunate the USB standard is the trend. Now depending on the available mouse and keyboard, connect them into the ports. For the PS/2 standard, the green (with a mouse symbol) is for the mouse, while the blue (with a keyboard symbol) is for the keyboard. See below:

3. **Connecting the Power Cables:** Both the Monitor and System Unit have their different Power supply cable, so connect each of them as the Power Supply cable is just the same.

**Power cable connected
to the Monitor**

**Power cable connected
to the System Unit**

 The cable is made to fit the ports, if it fails, do not force it.

WINDOWS AND DESKTOP INTRODUCTION

From our general introductory page, we explained Windows as a graphical user interface (GUI) component constituting of desktop environment that supports window managers' implementation, and provisions of basic function support to graphic hardware like mouse, keyboard, and others. It exists in various forms both in Application software such as Microsoft Excel, SPSS, App-XL, Firefox Mozilla, etc. Including in Programming Software, like Notepad, and as well as system windows of Windows OS such as the window of a Control panel or that of a Folder. Although regardless of their types, there are common features among them. These features are the Side bar, Scroll bar, Menu bar, and Display Control buttons. But, some distinguishing features are Tab, Ruler, Map, Gridline, Zoom, et cetera.

Common Features of Windows

1. **Title Bar:** It displays the name of an active Window.

2. **Display Control Buttons:** These are the buttons, which control the displaying of Windows. They are Maximize/Minimize button, Close button, and Restore button.

3. **Ribbon/Menu bar:** This is a bar holding all the Menus of Windows. A menu is a drop-down dialog box attached on the menu bar. It holds a list of commands, in which a user has options on the various command of actions to use. Now, since MS Office windows is based on versions, such as MS Office 2003, MS Office 2007, and others no longer use Menu bar, rather they are built with Ribbons that constitute different tabs. For example, MS Word in 2003, and MS Word 2007 are built with Menu and Ribbon bar respectively. Moreover, note that in MS Office 2007, and that of 2010, inside a Ribbon is located a tab(s), and inside a tab, we have tools.

4. **Tool bar:** This is a bar holding user's choice command tools. Tools for shortcut operations of the computer are placed on the tool bar.

5. **Address bar:** This is a bar, which indicates the address line of opened OS windows. But, in web browser window, it serves as a place to enter a website address.

6. **Scroll bar:** It is used in taking both up and down, including left and right viewing of Windows document. It is of two forms, which are Horizontal and Vertical Scroll bars. The Vertical Scroll bar is used for up and down viewing, while the Horizontal Scroll bar is for left hand and right hand side viewing.

7. **Status bar:** As we work with a particular window, the status bar stands as activity report bar, which displays the real-time information of the activities of the windows.

A Window of Microsoft Excel Application Software

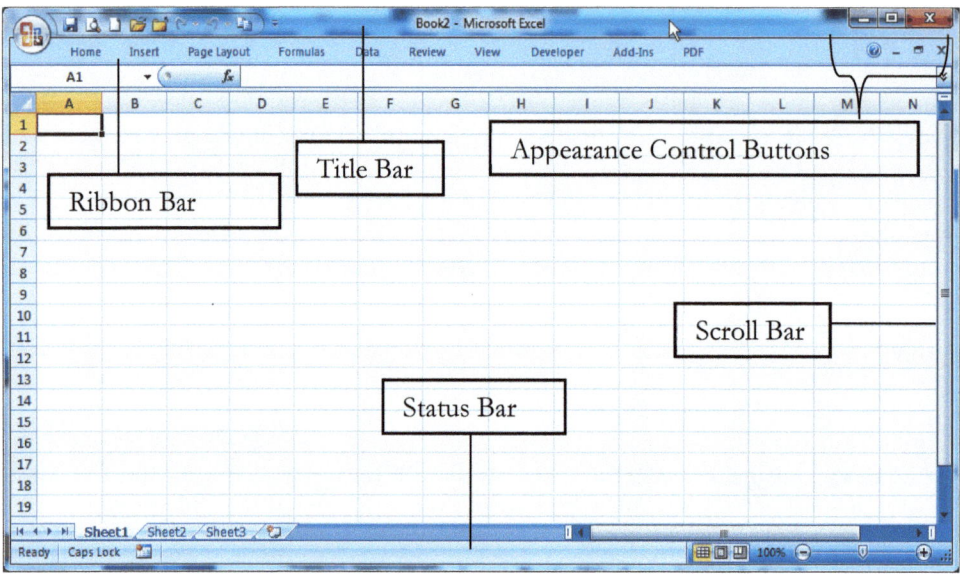

A Window of Windows OS

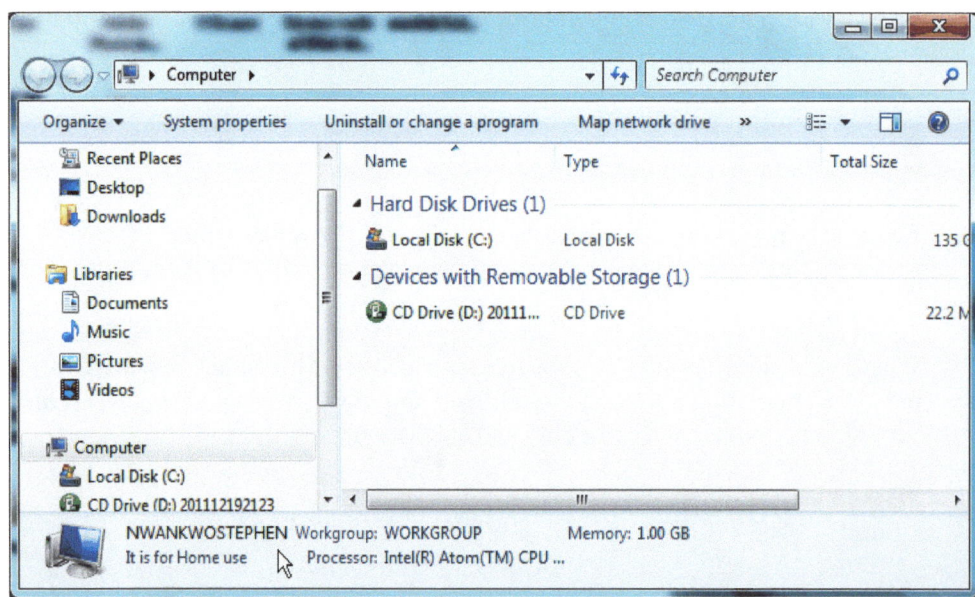

A Window of Firefox Mozilla Application Software

A Window of Programming Software, Notepad

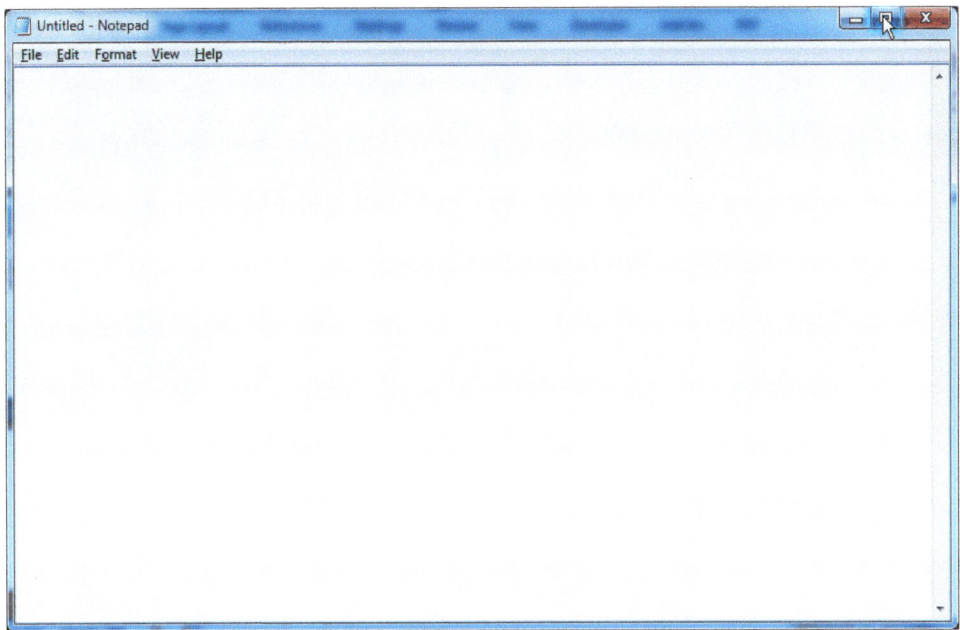

Note: The above programming window named **Notepad** is an environment that comes with Windows OS. For example, after Windows OS installation, we will have it.

EXPLORING THE DESKTOP ENVIRONMENT

A desktop environment is a location on a personal computer screen, which helps a user to get around and do work on a computer. It serves has an interactive platform where a user can perform shortcut activities when working with files and folders or icons on the computer.

Like its name, it is like a piece of office table with drawers where someone can carry out office table duties. In this aspect, the drawers are the folders, and books and other things are the files placed inside the drawers.

Usually, when we powered 'on' our computer and after the final booting (i.e. after the proper starts), the final appeared-screen of the computer is the computer desktop. So it is the main screen on the computer, and if no program or folder is open, the computer will display it. For example, the most common desktop environment on personal computers is the one given by Microsoft Windows, another common environment is the one given by Apple Mac OS X, and for a smart phone, it is the home screen.

A Microsoft Windows Desktop Environment

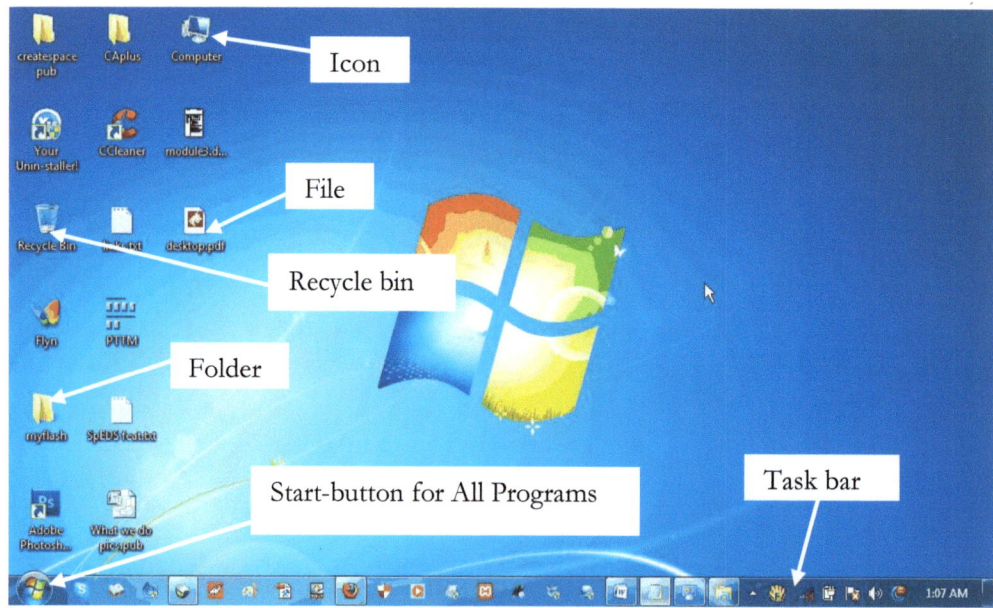

Dialog Box

Unlike the Windows environment where there are placed-commands for executing actions by the user, the Desktop environment does not have placed or listed commands on its environment that a user can use to operate its environment, rather it works with dialog boxes.

The dialog box is an unequal size box, bearing list of commands, which a user can use to carryout function on a computer desktop. Most of the actions perform on the desktop include folder creation, icons management, copy/cut and paste of file(s) from one folder to another, renaming of icon, and other actions.

Although, like we stated above, no place where commands can be found on a desktop environment, therefore, the only way to get a corresponded list of commands in order to carry out a particular action is by clicking on that particular object or icon. For example to create a folder, we place the mouse pointer on any part of the desktop (not on any icon), and click the right-hand-side (RHS) of the mouse, then follow the dialog boxes that will prompt out, and create a folder.

From the picture, by clicking the RHS of the mouse, the dialog box circled with '1' appears, and clicking on the command 'New', the sub-dialog box circled with '2' prompted, a move of the mouse pointer, and clicking of the 'Folder' command or image will create a folder bearing a default name of "New Folder", which can be renamed later.

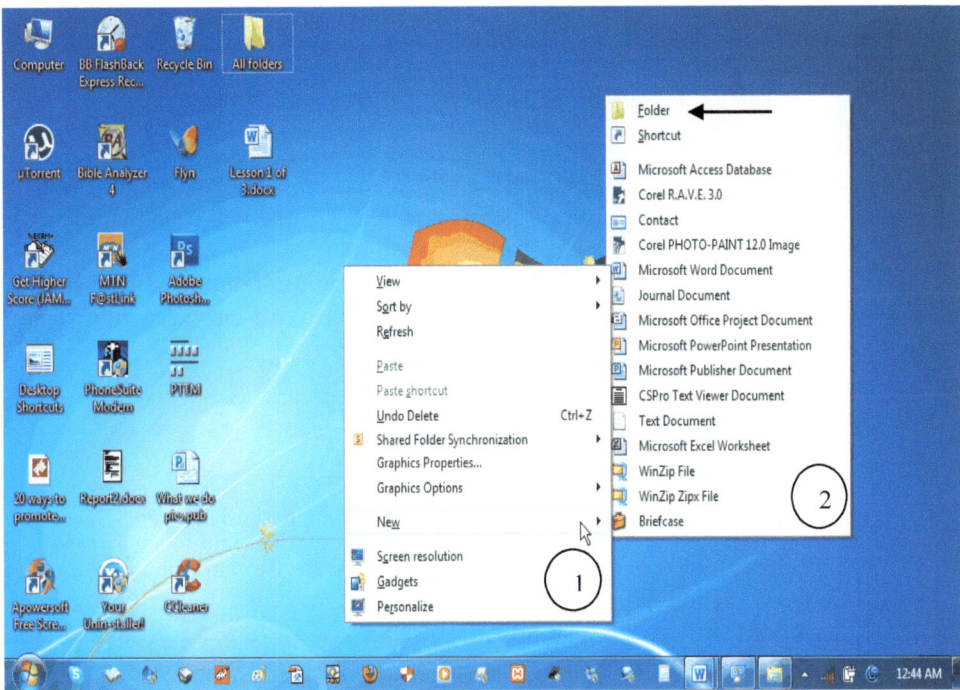

To rename or carryout any action on the Folder, we will place the mouse pointer on the Folder, and click the RHS of it in order to prompt a dialog box with a list of commands. See the below diagram; inside the dialog box, there are list of commands, including the 'Rename' command.

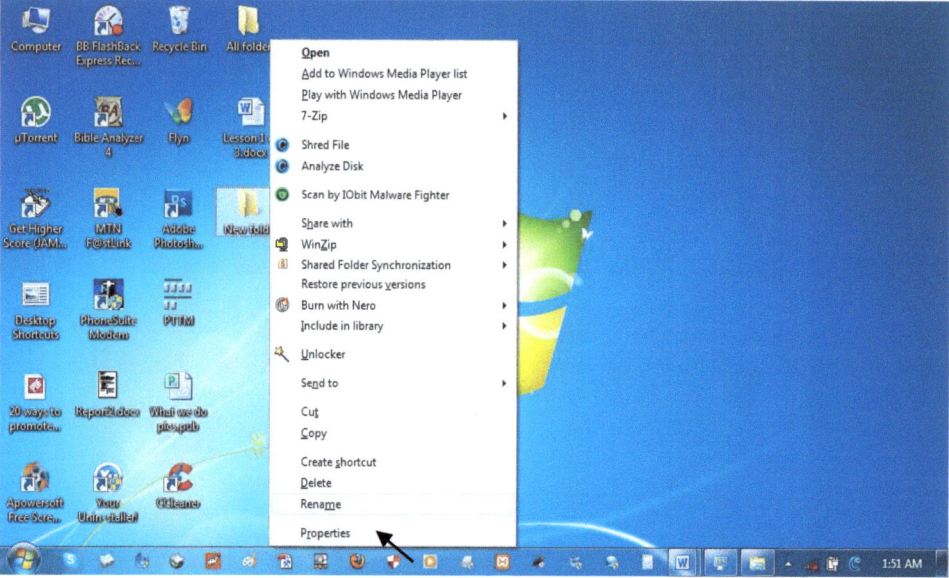

Recycle Bin

This is a dustbin place or garbage container where any file that is no longer needed and got deleted are kept for recovery purpose. When you delete a file, it is usually moved to the Recycle Bin so that you can restore the file later if you want.

To permanently remove files from your computer and reclaim any hard disk space they were using, you need to delete the files from the Recycle Bin. You can delete individual files from the Recycle Bin or empty the entire Recycle Bin at once.

- Click to open Recycle Bin.

- Do one of the following:

- To permanently delete one file, click it, press Delete, and then click Yes.

- To delete all of the files, right-clicking the Recycle Bin and then clicking Empty Recycle Bin, and then click Yes.

> **Note:** Any file deleted from the Recycle bin cannot be recovered, unless by the use a file recovery application software or program, such as **Recuva**, which is a file recovery software published by a software development company known as **Piriform Limited**.

Task bar

The taskbar is the long horizontal bar at the bottom of a powered computer desktop. It is the landing place of every opened work running on the desktop environment. For its primary function, every folder, file, or application running on the computer will always be located at the task bar, just for easy use. In other words, it serves as a status bar, there by highlighting the current tools or windows that we are working with. In addition, it is used to track the activity of open or active-windows and files, and as well as minimize, maximize, and restore them.

For location, following the way it (task bar) is been displayed on a desktop environment, it is located on the bottom of the desktop and can be adjusted to the left, right, or top depending on the user's choice. Although, this adjustment is not necessary as doing it may hinder or cover some displaying space of the desktop environment.

It has four sections, which are *Start-button*, the *Middle section*, *Notification area*, and *Show desktop section*. The *start-button* gives access to *Start-menu of All Programs*. The *middle section* shows the document file or program file a user has opened and/or pined, and as well allows the user to quickly switch among them. Thirdly is *the notification area*, which includes *a clock and icons* settings that communicate the status of certain active or working programs and computer settings, such as date and time. Lastly is the *show-desktop button*; a click on it will automatically minimize opened window(s) by showing the desktop environment. See below is a diagram of Task-bar with its sections. But, the features of pin/unpin files or program on the taskbar, and the show-desktop button are only found in Windows 7 and subsequent versions. They were not featured in Windows XP and its predecessors. For example, if you are using Windows 7 or any other higher version of Windows OS, you can pin/unpin a program or file by positioning the mouse pointer on the icon of that particular program, click the RHS of the mouser, and select either pin/unpin command that will prompt from the opened dialog box.

See pictures below:

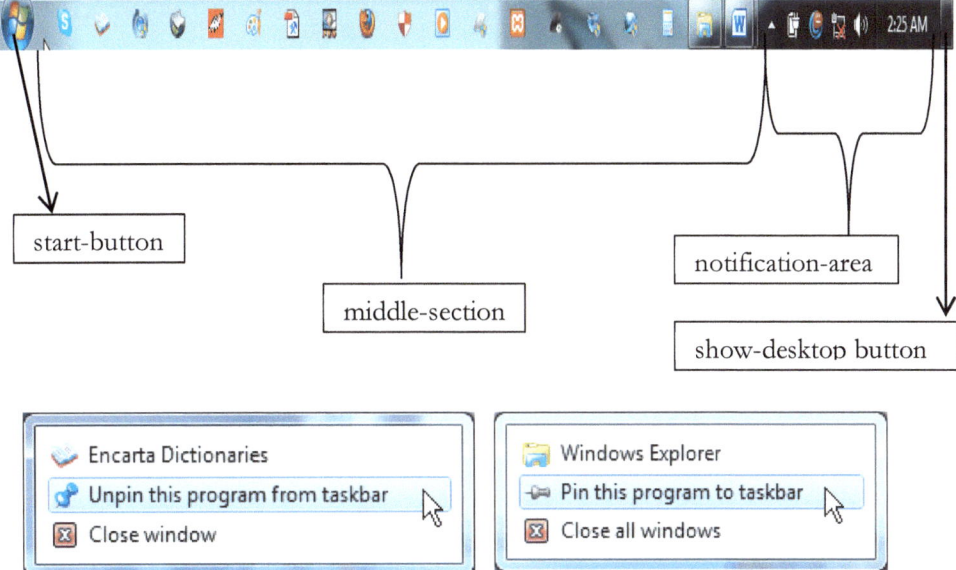

The '**Unpin**' is used for already pined program, while '**Pin**' is for not pined program or file.

Time and Date Settings

In setting date and time of a computer, we are to use the *Time and Date setting button* located in the *Notification area* of the Taskbar. The button is always there, displaying the real-time of the computer. To use it; we only click on it, and then follow up the information of the dialog box that will appear.

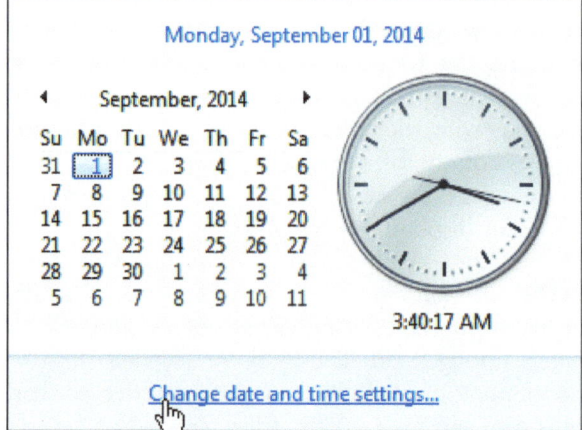

For the taskbar, it is associated with a *Windows Task Manager*, and a click at the RHS of the bar will prompt a dialog window with indication of its command (i.e. windows task manager command). For usage, its advance use will help in managing both closing and other activities of current programs. For instance, to close a particular program, which is not running properly, click on the RHS of the mouse, from the dialog box, click "*Select the Task Manager*", in the Windows Task Manager, select the program to be close, and click "End task".

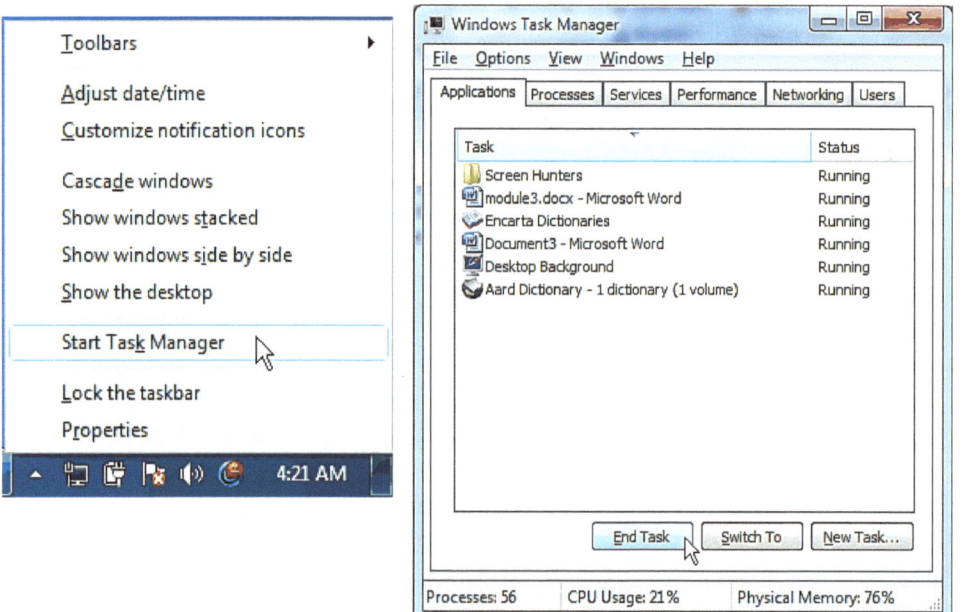

Desktop Actions

A User can arrange the desktop items, and do other activities in order to make the desktop look good, or make job easy. For instance, a click at the RHS of the mouse pointer on any part of the desktop (except on the file, folder, status bar, starts-button, or icon) will prompt a right-hand dialog box, and the position of the mouse pointer on the 'View' command will open an attached-dialog box of the View command.

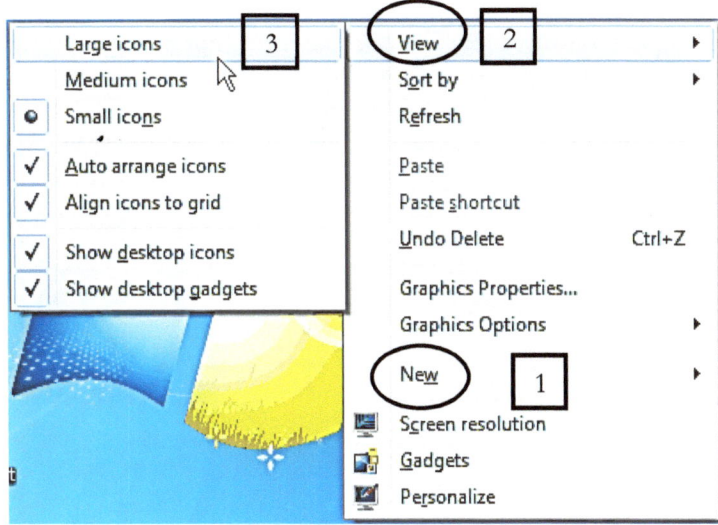

Folder:

In a discussion of file systems, a folder (also called Directory in MS DOS) is often create in order to use it for file management. In other words, it is a package box whereby many computer files can be place in it, either by individual as single standing files or by group with sub-folder(s). For instance, in Windows file management, folders are used in arranging files according to their purpose through their different names for easy location and identification. They are classified as *Root folder, Parent folder, Sub-folder,* and *Active or Working-folder.*

Root folder is the folder that holds all the folders in a computer. While folders can parent each other, root folder cannot be hold by any other folder. A good example is the Local/Hard Disk folder, whose picture image is a box icon.

For another, Parent folder is a folder holding another folder known as Sub-folder, or even files. A Sub-folder can hold another folder(s) known as Sub-sub-folder(s), and this can be in continuity, depending on how many folders the user intends to create. In this manner, an Active-folder is the folder in which its file or application is in use.

For folder creation, to create a folder at the desktop, as we expressed above, we only click the RHS of the mouse pointer on any part of the desktop, (except on the file, folder, status bar, starts-button, or icon) and this will prompt a right-hand dialog box, positioning the mouse pointer on the 'New' listed among in the dialog box will open an attached box that will enable us to select a 'folder'. But, in the application of Command Prompt, the name a 'folder' is called directory. So Root, Parent, Sub-folder, and Active folder are called Root directory, Parent directory, Sub-directory, and Active-directory respectively.

Icon

An icon in the concept of computing is a picture, which usually stands as a shortcut for a program, file, folder, or an action for a program to do. In another way, it is an image picture representing a shortcut of a folder or application software. A folder located on a desktop of a computer is called an icon, but with an opened-book icon. Similarly, application software when placed on a desktop stands as a shortcut for accessing the software is also called icon.

For usage, icons are used in many places on a computer. For instance, the desktop environment contains icons as shortcuts, and double-clicking on any of them will open up the file, folder, or application that particular one stand for. For example in Microsoft Windows, the desktop will often have an icon for the *Recycle Bin*, which is usually looks like *Trash Can*, and a double-click, will open it. Moreover, for icon management, pictures of icons can be change, depending on the user, who has the right to change it. Most times, we may decide to change the picture of an icon or a folder in order to suit the content of it. This is to make us remember easily what is in that icon. For instance, let us do this activity by changing the icon of a folder named 'global'.

Activity:
1. Create a folder with a name 'global' on your desktop,
2. Select the folder by clicking the RHS of your mouse,
3. Select the "properties command",

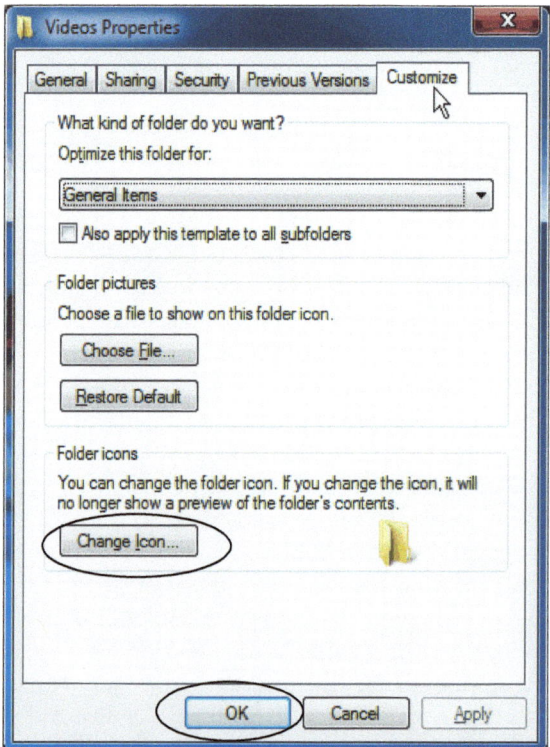

4. Click the Customize button, then the "Change Icon", and the OK button.
5. A new dialog box will open, then scroll, and select a global icon picture or image, and finally click OK.

Default Folders of a Computer

Default folders are folders created automatically by a computer for the purpose of proper file storage and easily identification. For instance, whether in a reformatted or brand new computer, the default folders are there, for the user to store related files in them. In other words, they came with the computer as we bought or reformatted them, and are used for various purposes.

By *parent folders*, they are *Favorites*, which holds the Desktop, Downloads, and *Recent Places* *shortcuts*. The *Libraries parent folder* that holds the *Documents, Pictures, Music, and Videos folders*. The *Computer parent folder* holds the Local Disk folders, and exists as the environment where every Disk plugged or inserted will be identified via the displaying of the related drive. Then finally the *Network Folder*, which will displayed every network connected folder with other computers.

By usage, if you are working on a computer, and be clicking folders, the *Recent Places folder* by default shows the recent folders you have visted. The *Desktop folder* below the *Recent Places folder* represent a shortcut to the desktop environment. Giving it a 'click' will display all the icons, sub-folders, and files placed as shortcut on the it (i.e. desktop environment). The *Download folder* by default keeps every file or application software download from Online.

The *Libraries* holds the *Document folder*, which keeps every document of the computer, and as well serves as a place where application software or program folders are also kept for purpose of saving their files. For example, if you installed an SPSS (Statistical Packages for Social Sciences) application program, it will automatically create a folder named SPSS, where its files will be prompt to be save. Others are *Pictures, Music,* and *Videos folders*, which are used for keeping picture, music, and video files respectively.

Although holding the *Local Disk folder*, every other external disk that is inserted will be as an icon under the parent folder of the Computer Folder.

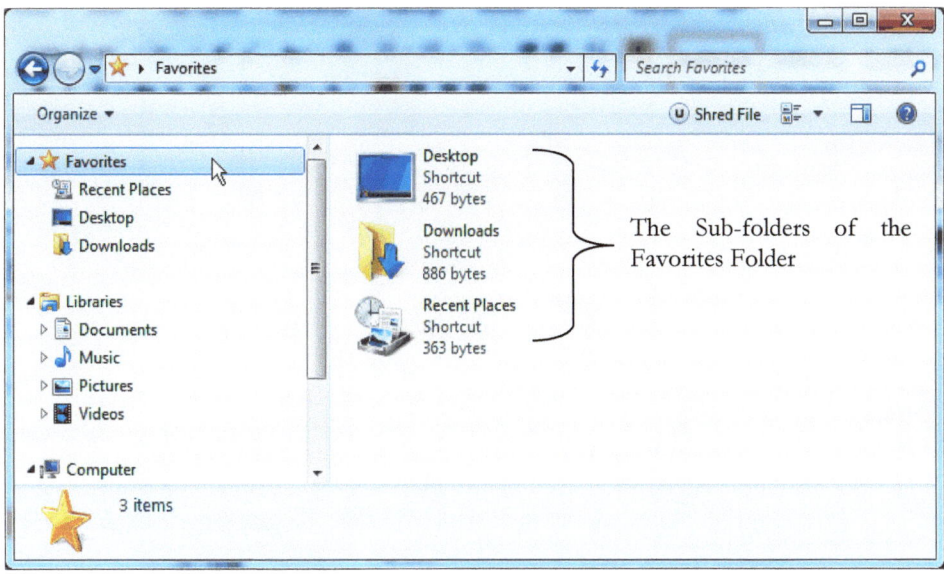

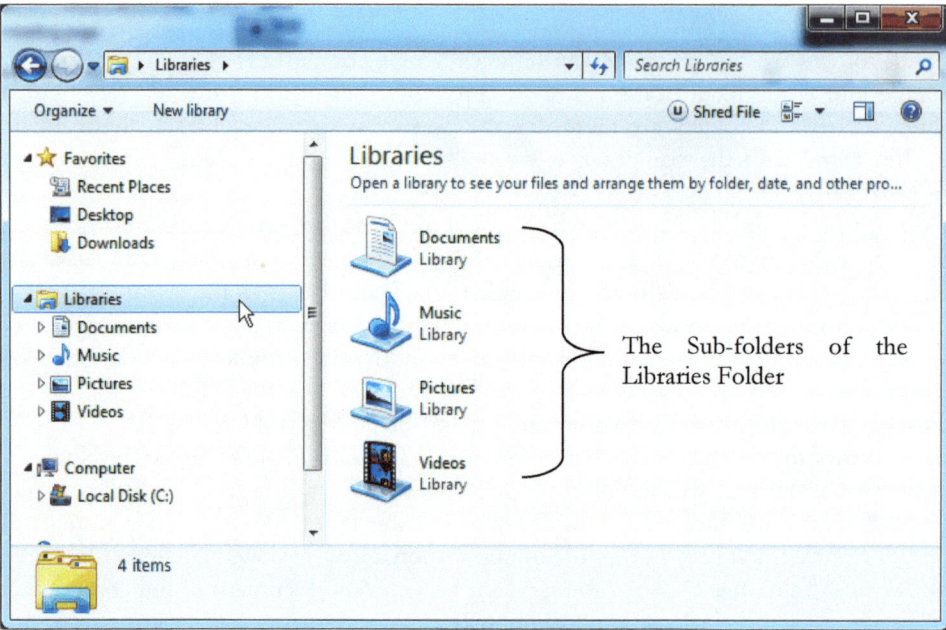

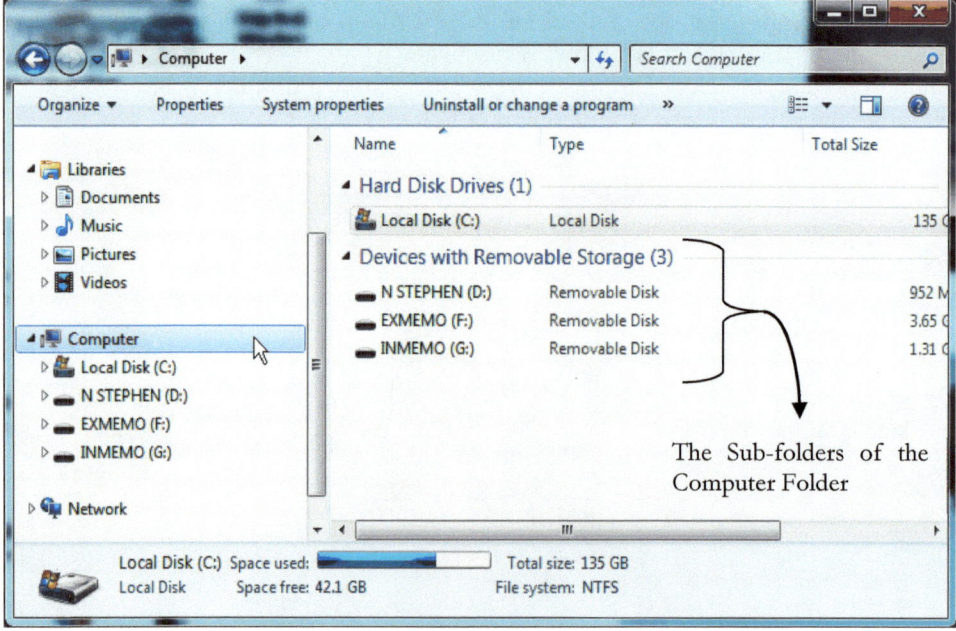

In the same manner, a click of the the *Network Folder* will also display the connected folders. But, if the computer is not network connected, it will display a message for such.

The Local Disk

The Local Disk (the computer hard disk) is been displayed by a click on the *Computer folder/link* that is displayed on the *start-box* of the Start-button.

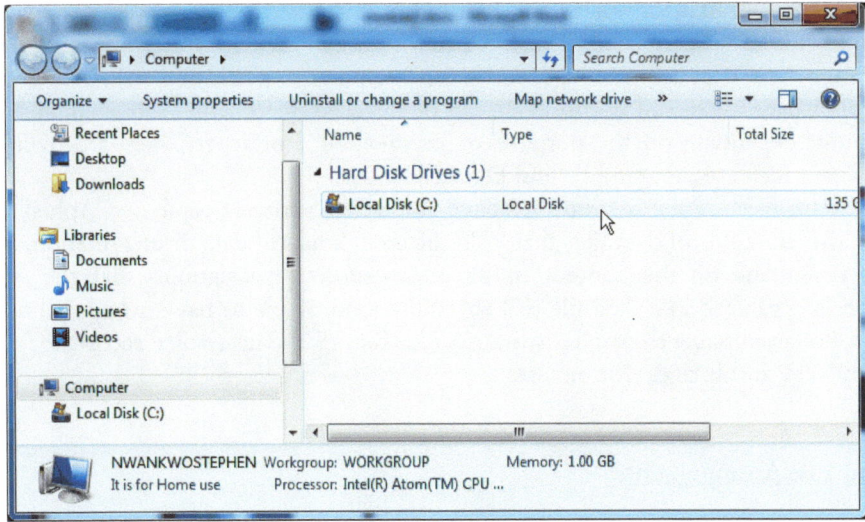

Most of the computer disk is always partitioned with other drives, such as E-Drive in order to have a backup Local Disk for the computer. Operationally, at a click of the Local Disk, we have access to all the Windows files, programs, and other Application programs installed in the computer. But to avoid damage, it is not advisable for us to delete or explore the hard disk, except for advance level use. See below, opened local disk of **nwankwostephen computer**:

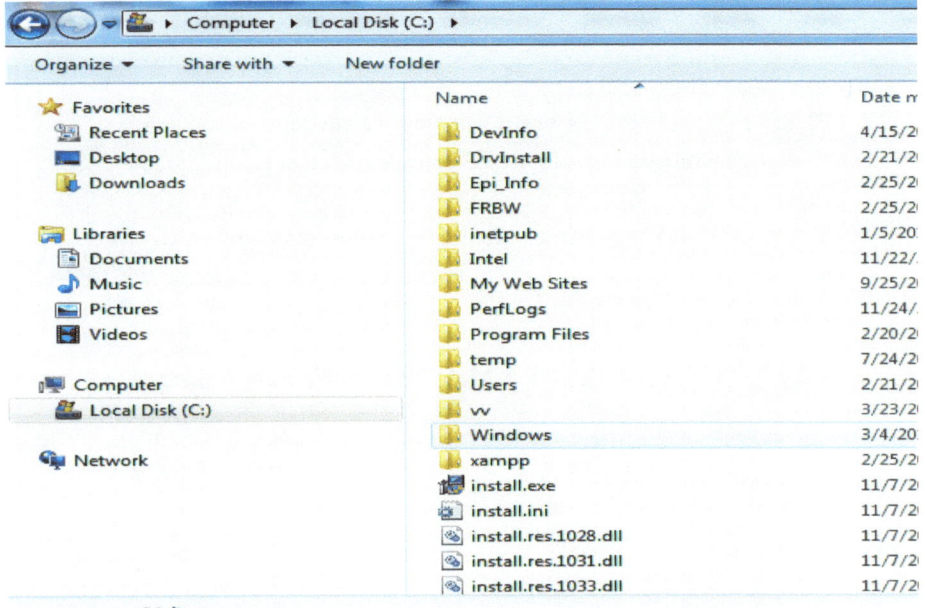

About Computer File

In computer, different tasks are performed as a result of different computer files. In this aspect, Windows as the case at hand is made up as one of them where tasks are performed with various files. But first, what is a computer file?

Computer file is a container of related information created for computer uses, or computer user uses. That is, it can be used by the computer to perform a task, or it is created by a computer user for record purposes. It can be installed, read, write, retrieved, and stored in a computer depending on the purpose of its creation. For types, there are mainly two forms of files, which are program file and Data files.

The program files are the software we have studied in Software topic of CAplus-1 book. There are different kinds of data files that hold different kinds of data or information. So data file varies depending on the content of its information. This signifies that the way the information is organized in a data file will show the kind of file to have, which is known as file format. For example, we have Text files, Audio files (for songs, voice recordings), Video files (for movies), and Images (for pictures).

Folder and File Arrangement

For quick accessibility or location of a file in a computer, it is necessary to arrange all accepted and created files into their respective folders. Following our early teaching about folder, we need to create a folder with a name relating to the type of file we will keep inside it. For instance, files are to keep in their respective default folders, which we have learnt. But, if the folder of a file is not found in the default folders, then we create new folder. But such folder, if it is for document purpose should be place inside the default Document folder as sub-folder.

> ### Note:
>
> 1. Please do not open the Local Disk, or save any kind of file inside it.
> 2. If you download any file from Internet, check it on the Download folder.
> 3. Create sub-folders for files that have other units. For example, files bearing the names of students in particular classroom can have a folder, with sub-folders. Such folders can be as below:
>
> ### Classroom Folder > Male Folder, Female Folder
>
> To access any of the folder, say the *Female Folder*, we first open the *Classroom folder*, and then open the Female Folder. The same is to that of the *Male Folder*.

Desktop Icons, File Privacy, and Computer Speed

The desktop environment of a computer needs to be maintained in order to help the processing speed of the computer. To maintain desktop environment, a user has to allow few shortcuts of icons on the environment. This can be done by creating parent folders and sub-folders on the desktop, and use them to pack most of the shortcut icons inside them. The reason is that leaving too much icons on a desktop will affect the booting or processing speed of the computer. This is because in the booting period of the computer, all the desktop icons must be displayed before the user can begin any work with the computer. In most cases, the icons may be displaying one after another, thereby keeping the user at a longer waiting. Similar case is of the same, when sometime a user may try to open a file or application software via the desktop.

Furthermore, another disadvantage is that most people often create shortcuts of MS Office files, for example, MS Word and placed them on their desktop. Truly, files exposed at this condition do not have privacy because they are been exposed via the filenames. Take for instance, an Accountant who prepared a file containing the list of Employees and their salary earnings, and saved it with a relative filename, such as "*employees salaries.xlsx*"; if this file is placed directly on the desktop, its privacy will be limited. This is because anybody that looked directly at the desktop will see, and quickly figure out that such document is in that computer. For better, if for instance, the desktop has a desktop folder, the file will be put inside it, and this will limit the direct view of the file.

A Computer Desktop filled with many icons

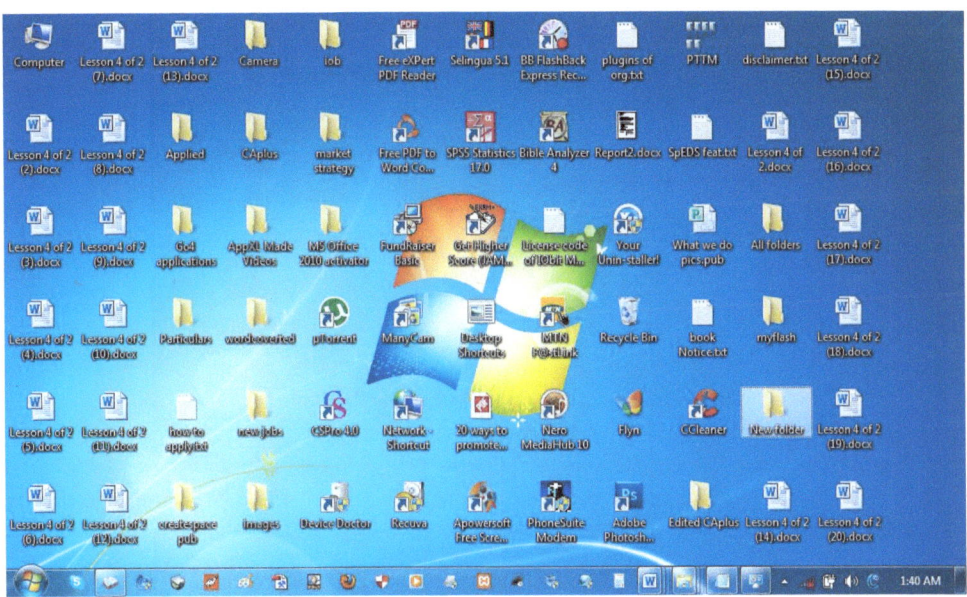

Start-Button

As we mentioned earlier, the Task bar has three sections, which are *Start-button*, the *Middle section*, and the *Notification area*. If we click Start-button, it will give access to its *Start-menu of All Programs*, and other sufficient commands and tools of the Windows, such as Computer folder, Document folder, Windows help and support place, and others. For example, see below, a click on Start-button of Windows 7:

Circled and pointed by the mouse pointer is the *Start-button*, and a clicked on it; shows files, program tools, applications, and folders. Most of the folders, files, applications, and programs tools are shortcut, thereby representing their main bodies. At a click of the button, the *All Programs* directory opens the list of all the programs installed in the computer, the *Computer folder* shows the available disks, such as the Local Hard Disk of the computer, while the *Documents* shows the recent documents or files that the user were working on. In addition, each of the items gives access to its location.

> **Note**: Once a user observes the above Start-button, the person can still use that of other Windows, including that of Windows 8.

BRIEF ABOUT WINDOWS ACCESSORIES

Although, been treated in the hardware and software topics of CAplus-1 and 2, the term 'accessory' in computing means "functional-support" in which we have an accessory hardware that support the functional running of a computer. As a form of hardware, it is indirectly connected to the computer, and without it, computer can still work, but may lack efficiency base on the user. A good example is UPS.

In a likely manner, *Windows Accessories* are the application programs, and system tools that we use to perform some activities (e.g. maintenance) of Windows in our computer. They are accessories, but to that of software, and functionally support the works of Windows, and are to be used by the user for Windows maintenance and repair.

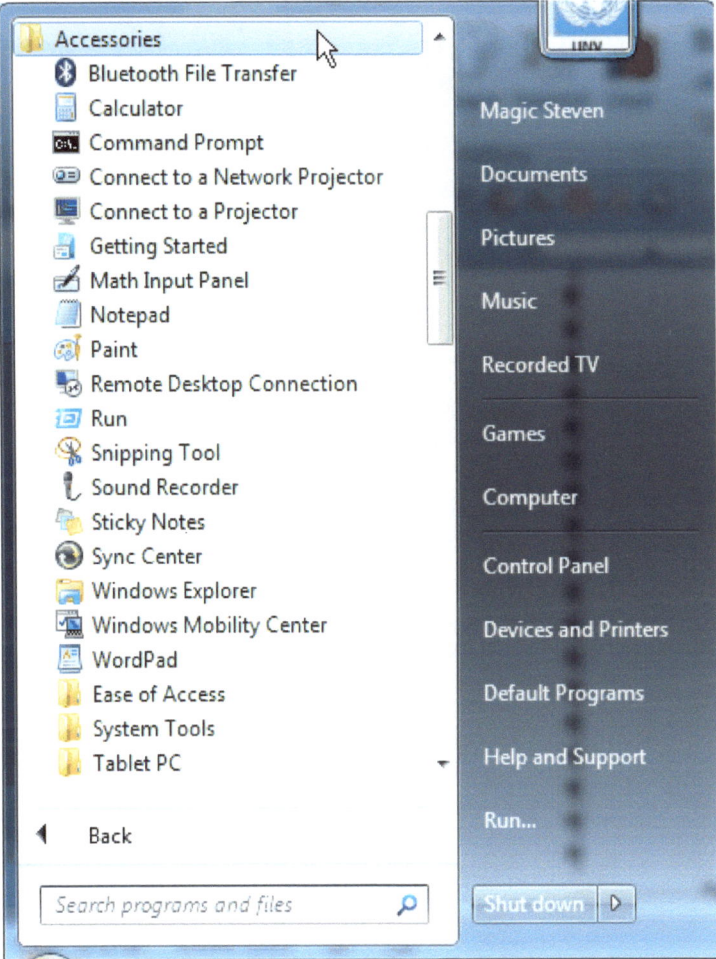

Note: Once a user observes the above Windows Accessories, the person can still use that of other Windows, including that of Windows 8.

System Tools

Although, there are many applications and tools of the Windows Accessories, but we only referred to *system tools*, and *command prompt application* due to their recognition in Windows computer. Similarly, understand that System tools are also known as Utility tools. See 'Utilities' topic in CAplus-1.

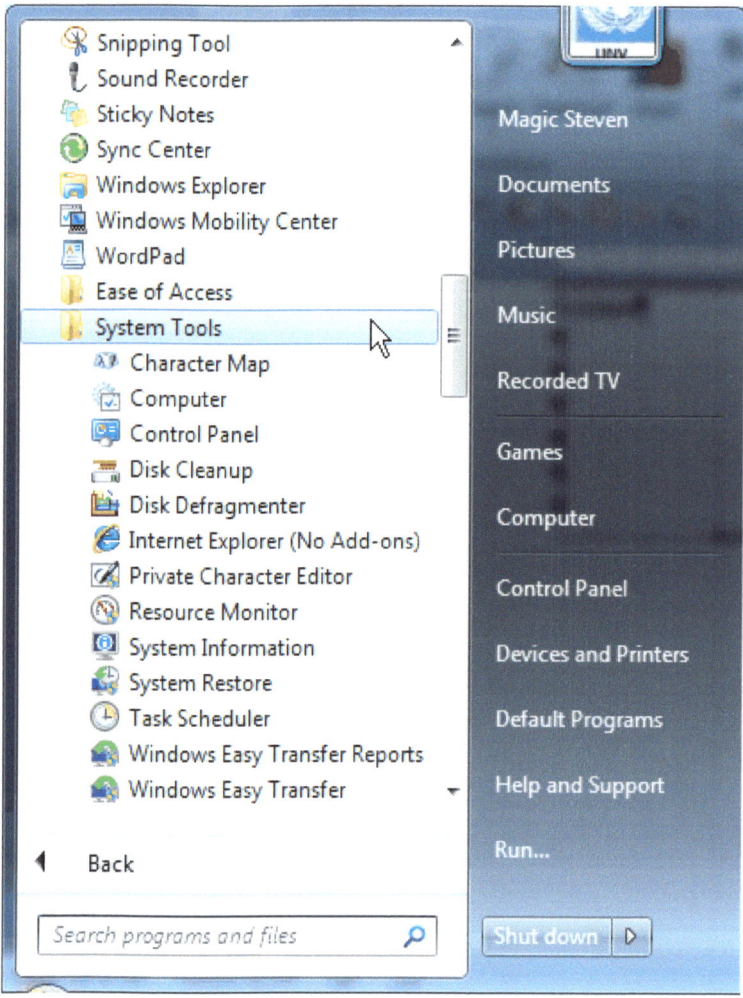

Note: Once a user observes the above Windows Accessories, the person can still use that of other Windows, including that of Windows 8.

INTRODUCTION TO WINDOWS CONTROL PANEL

The Control Panel been an inherent part of Microsoft Windows Operating System is a part of the Microsoft Windows graphical user interface which allows users to view and manipulate basic system settings and controls through applets (i.e. a single computer program that performs single task), such as adding and removing software, controlling user accounts, changing accessibility options, and others.

To access a Control Panel both in Windows 7, 8, and Windows XP, do the followings:

1. Click the START-BUTTON

2. Click ALL PROGRAMS

3. Scroll and Click ACCESSORIES

4. Click SYSTEM TOOLS, and

5. Click the CONTROL PANEL

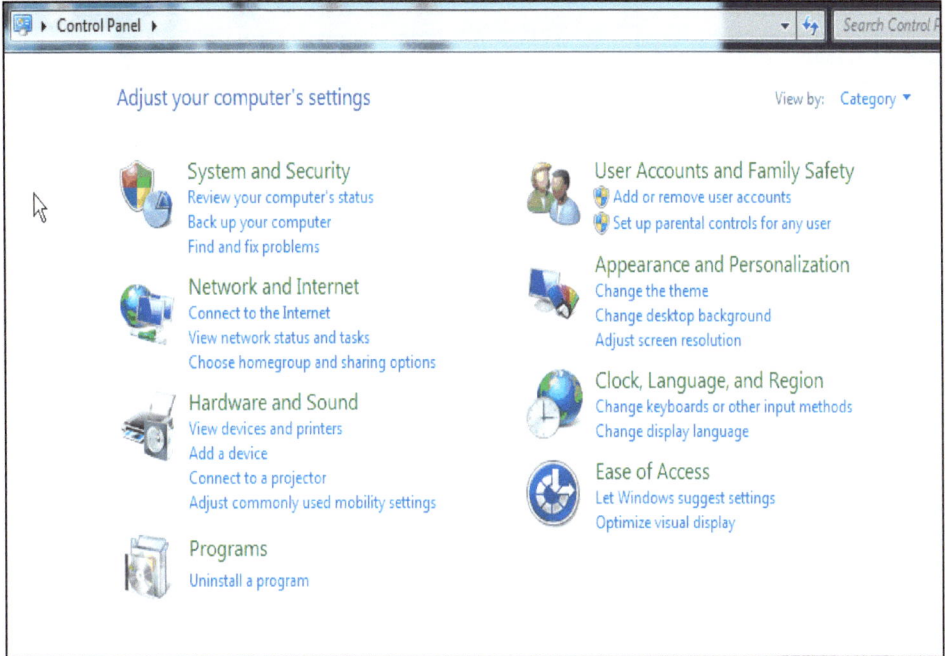

From the above, the diagram is of a Control Panel of Windows 7. It has eight categories, which are *System and Security, Network and Internet, Hardware and Sound, Programs, User Accounts and Family Safety, Appearance and Personalization, Clock, Language, and Region,* and finally, *Ease of Access.* Although, this is similar to that of Windows XP categories, which is of nine categories, (See the next page). But by operation, if a user can explore the last diagram above (which is Windows 7 Control Panel), the person can as well explore other Windows, including that of Windows 8, XP, and Vista.

Category	Use to:
Appearance and Personalization	• Change the theme • Change desktop background • Adjust screen resolution
Clock, Language, and Region	• Change keyboard, and other input method • Change display language
Ease of Access	• Let Windows suggest settings • Optimize visual display
Hardware and Sound	• View devices and printers • Add a device • Connect to a projector • Adjust commonly used mobility settings
Network and Internet	• Connect to the internet • View network status and tasks • Choose homegroup and sharing options
Programs	• Uninstall a program
System and Security	• Review your computer's status • Back up your computer • Find and fix problems
User Accounts and Family safety	• Add and remover user account • Set up parental control for any user

Note: *Once a user observed the above Control Panel, the person can still use Vista, Windows 7, XP, and 8.*

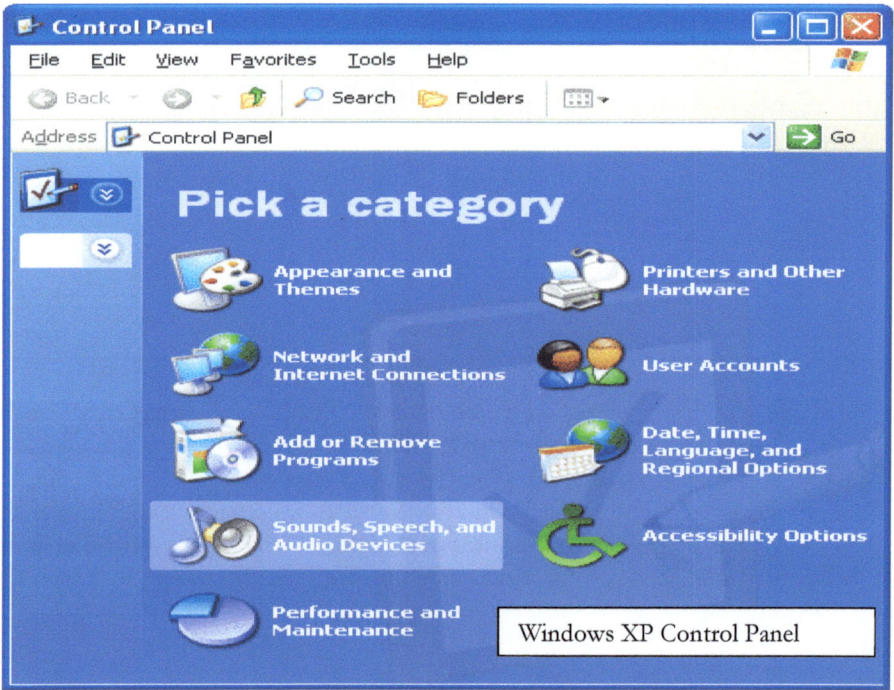

Windows XP Control Panel

INTRODUCTION TO COMMAND PROMPT APPLICATION

Briefly, Command Prompt is a command line interpreter application which is available in most Windows operating systems. It is called Windows Command Processor or Command Shell, despite been incorrectly called DOS (Disk Operating System). It is a Windows program, which emulates many of the command line abilities available in MS-DOS (Microsoft DOS), but it is not actually MS-DOS.

For usage, it is used to execute typed-in or entered commands, including; the execution of batch files, perform advance administrative functions and troubleshooting, and well as solve certain kinds of Windows issues; like the removing of Trojan or Virus from the computer, which some Antivirus cannot actually remove.

To use *command prompt*, a user must enter a valid command without or with inclusion of parameter(s), if there is a need, and *command prompt* will execute the command by performing the required task in the computer. In carrying out its function, the application is built with a large number of commands, but their availability differs from one operating system to another. Although, in order to access a *command prompt*, we only have to open the Windows Accessories directory through the Start-button, for instance, clicking on *Start, All Programs, Accessories,* and then the *command prompt.* And to exit from its environment, we only type *'exit'* and press the *'Enter*-key' located on the Keyboard.

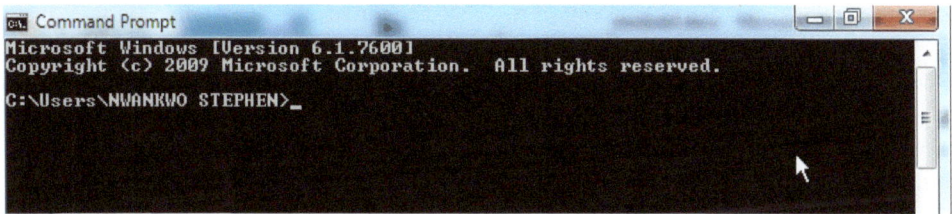

Moreover, as we expressed above, the application has several commands, which their validity depends on accurate syntax line usage. For example, see some common commands.

Commands and Commands with Parameters	Use to:
ATTRIB	Displays or Changes file attributes
ATTRIB –H –R –S (folder name)	This will unhide the attributes of the named folder, and make it possible for deleting.
CD	Display the name or Change the Current directory.
CD..	Close an open directory, and return to the Parent directory.
CD\	Close all open directories, and return to the Root directory, which is C:\>
CHKDSK	Check a disk and reports its status
DEL	Del one or more Files
DIR	Displays a list of files and Sub-directories in a Directory.
DIR/AH	Displays a list of files and Sub-directories in a Directory including Hidden files and Directory
HELP	Provides help information for Windows commands.
MD	Creates a directory or folder

Activity: *If you are in the Command Prompt environment, type 'Help', to know more.*

INTRODUCING MS OFFICE SUITES AND APPLICATIONS

Microsoft Office

By Microsoft Office (MS Office), we are referring to Desktop publishing Suites and Application software of Microsoft Corporation. Although, there are other desktop publishing applications that are for the same purpose like that of MS Office, especially the Open-Office-Org developed by Sun Micro System, but, MS Office is the most widely used.

For task application, each of the MS Office package is developed as an Application program used for specific task accomplishment. For instance, **MS Office Word 2010** serves as a Word Processor that we can use to create a professional-looking document with its comprehensive set of tools designed for document creation and formatting. In the other words, we use MS Word in every computer application work that requires word processing. Like a plain document, we write text in alignment or paragraph, and edit them whether for letter writing, book publication, or other purposes. Moreover, apart from MS Word are MS Excel, PowerPoint, Publisher, Project Planner, Outlook, MS Access, et cetera.

The **MS Excel** is a Spreadsheet, and a spreadsheet is a computer program that imitates a paper worksheet. It shows a large sheet (like a sheet of paper) that has many cells in a grid of rows and columns. Users can put words, sounds, images, or numbers into the cells in order to make headings and store information. The primary reasons for spreadsheets are for data analysis, calculation, and graph presentation. It is developed in a way whereby it is used to add up or subtract amounts on a bill, calculate sales tax, payroll, do statistical works, and other calculative and analytical works, including that of natural sciences and engineering. How it works, depend on its built-in program, which does all the math, and people only need to give the correct information via data entry. For chart presentation, spreadsheet used to produce diagrams, like graphs and pie charts for data representation based on data entry, and can perform routine works.

The **MS PowerPoint** is a graphical package that imitates paper document used for graphical designs. It shows a document where graphical works such as drawing, graphic-text design, and others can be done. It is a strong graphical page like CorelDraw.

The **MS Publisher** is the business publishing program used to create, design, and publish professional-looking marketing and communication materials. We can create materials for printing, and e-mail-use, and well as a simple website with an intuitive. It has task-based environment that can guide users from initial concept to final delivery of some simple professional design graphics. Although, being a graphic and word-pressing package or program, we can also perform the work of drawing, and as well, word processing just like it is done in the simplest primary works of MS PowerPoint and MS Word respectively. Broadly for graphic, it is the simplest place to design cards such as calendar, banner, certificate, catalog, letter heading, greeting cards, and others. To design a particular card, a user has to select customized card, and add information on it.

The **MS Outlook** is a Microsoft email client, which is used in managing email, both offline and online. It provides us with a comprehensive time and information management. Using new features such as *Instant Search* and *the To-Do Bar*, we can organize and instantly locate the information that we need. It has calendar sharing capabilities, Microsoft Exchange technology, and improved access to Microsoft Windows SharePoint Services information that can enable user, to safely share data that is stored in Office Outlook with coworkers, friends, and family, no matter where those people are located. It makes it easier for us to prioritize and control our time, allowing us to focus on the things that matter most.

The **MS Access** is a database application program of Microsoft Office. A database is a data management system for organizing collected data. In this manner, there will be a collection of raw data that can be manipulated, sorted, and queried in order to produce information. The data can be stored in many ways, and one of the ways is through computer. Fortunately, MS Access is one of the application programs to manage data as electronic database.

For composition, it shows a large datasheet (but in the appearance of table) that has many fields in a grid of rows and columns. Users can put words, sounds, images, or numbers into the fields of the table in order to make headings and store information. The data stored can be sorted, manipulated, and queried in order to produce information. The primary reasons for MS Access database are for data management, collecting, storing, sorting, querying, and analysis. In addition, it serves as a *Table creation tool* used for database creation, *Form development tool* used for displaying important fields that are created in the table, and Report preparation tool used for report preparation.

Furthermore, is the last, but not the least, **MS Project Planner**, which is MS Office Application that can help us to effectively manage and prioritize projects and resources across organizations. With the program, we can efficiently plan all types of works, manage project resources effectively, gain insight and visibility of the project in ongoing processes, therefore, communicate and collaborate at ease with the project. By application, it is mostly used by project managers in ongoing projects.

MS Project Planner, 2007 Interface

MS Word 2010Interface

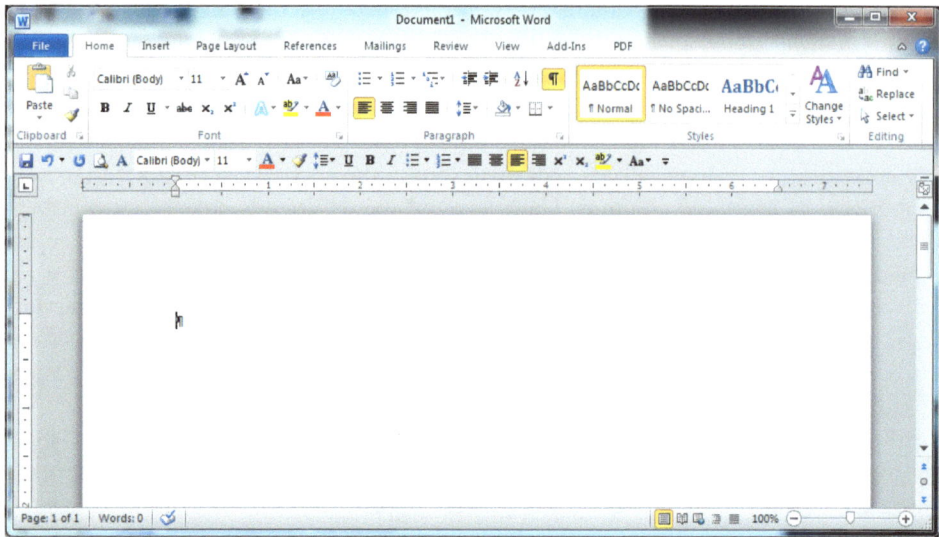

MS Excel 2010 Interface

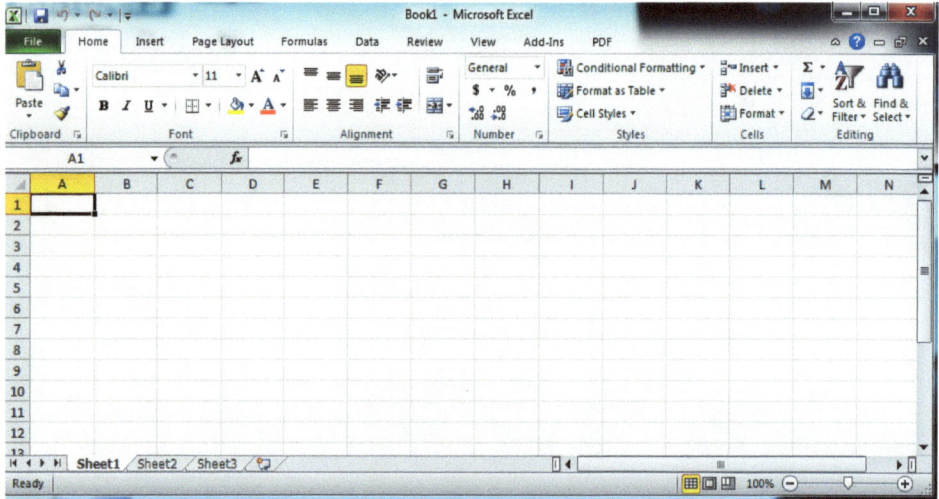

MS PowerPoint 2010 Interface

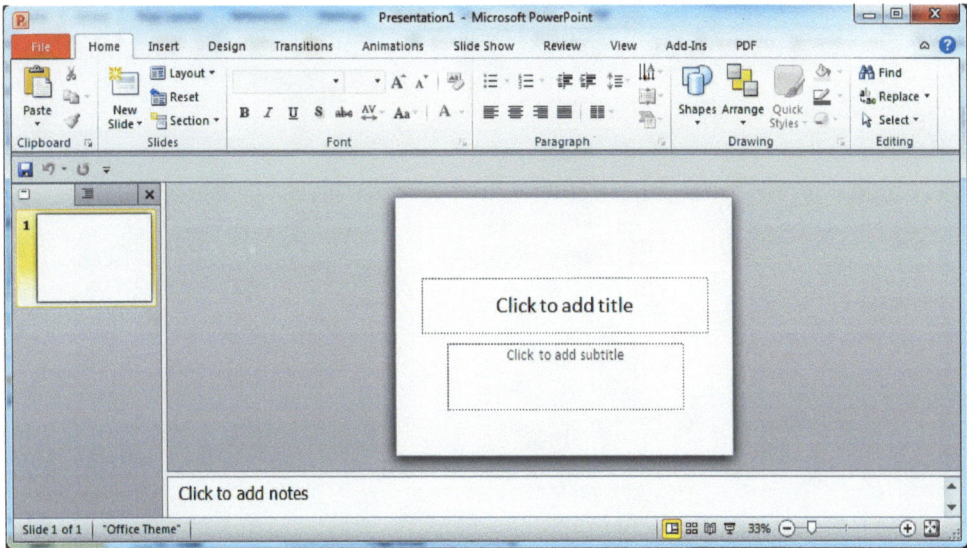

MS Publisher 2010 Interface

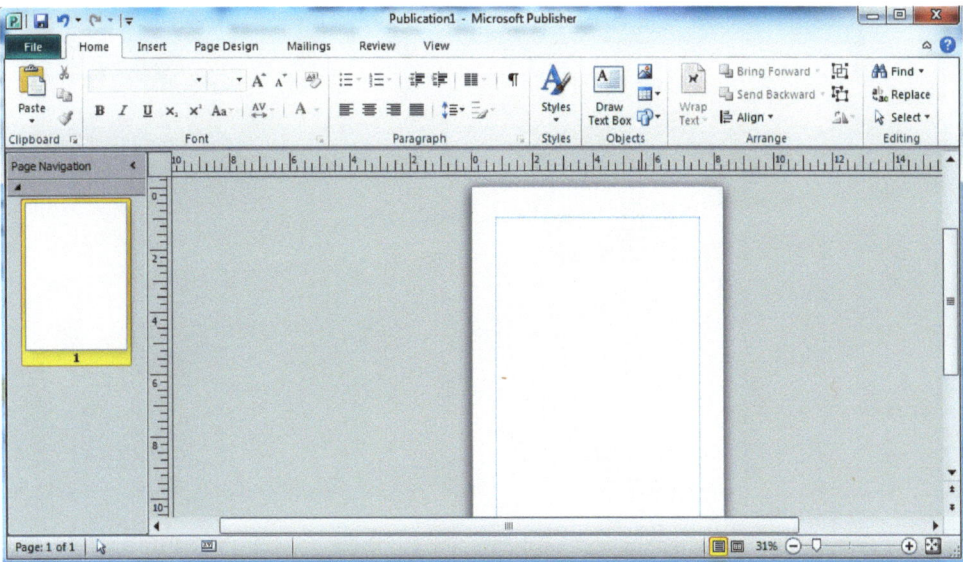

MS Outlook 2010 Interface

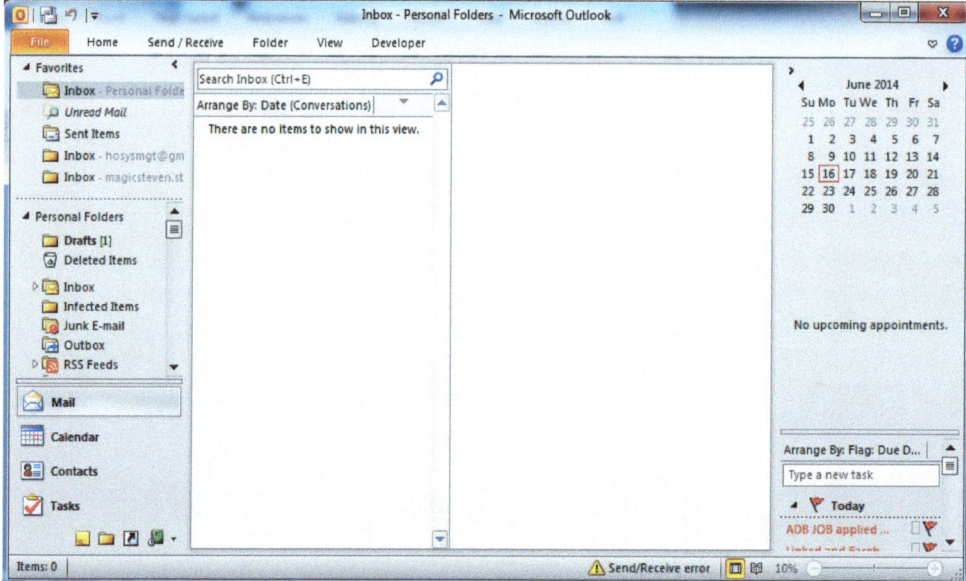

MS Access 2010 Interface

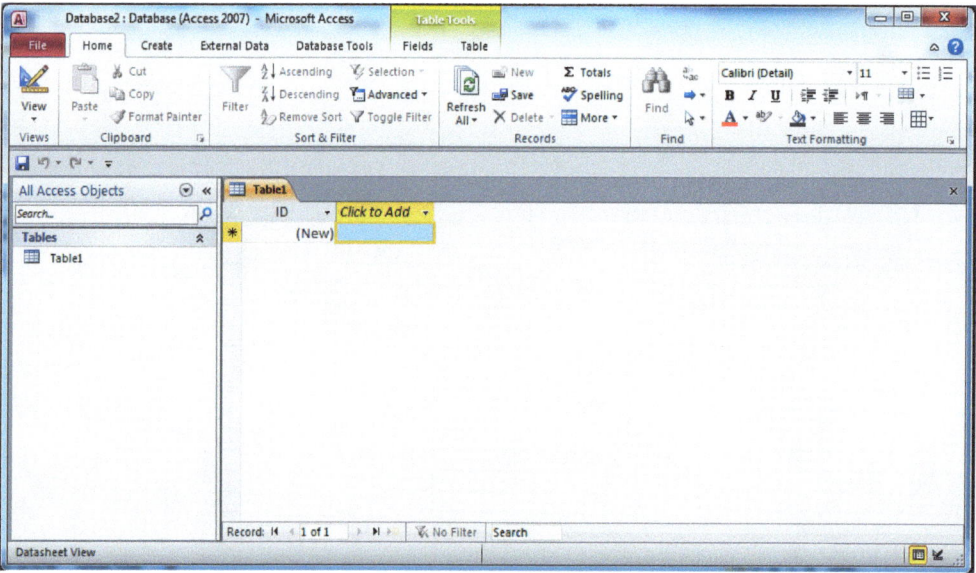

For the entire MS Office packages displayed above, their applications and uses required a formal training from organizations that can provide such service. Except, MS Project Planner, which is Microsoft Application, in most places we can train the others (i.e. the Microsoft Suites) together, either in certification or diploma programme. The training can be of three or six months duration, depending on add-on or other attached application programs. However, MS Project Planner is more of a professional program, and required a special single-training. For instance, an individual, who intends learning it, must have acquired computer knowledge, and the same way is MS Outlook.

BRIEF OF CHARACTER, BIT, BYTE, DATA, AND INFORMATION

There is a formation relationship among character, bit, byte, data, and information. Take for instance, it is a group of bit that formed byte, byte formed data, and data formed information. So by bit, we are referring to the smallest unit of characters. In this aspect, a character is a bit, but smallest when there are characters.

In computing language, character is one of the basic elements that make up a text file or data, therefore meaning that data known as datums (in plural) or datum (in singular) are group of characters. Then a group of meaningful data formed information.

	Meaning	**Examples**
Bit	A character or the smallest unit of characters.	C
Byte	A particular group of bits, say 8bits equals to a byte.	CAplus-1
Data	A group of characters or bytes.	*CAplus-1 is * a Computer Instructing book
Information	A group of meaningful data	CAplus-1 is Computer Instructing Book.

Data Measurement

As a group of characters, data are measurable, and so far as they are measurable, therefore we can measure files. For example a music file of 3.7MB, document file of 3,555KB, picture file of 4.2MB, and video file 3.3GB. Below are the measuring units of data:

Units	Values	Symbol
Bits		
Byte	Tenths	B
Hectobyte	Hundredths	HB
Kilobyte	Thousandths	KB
Megabyte	Millions	MB
Gigabyte	Billions	GB
Terabyte	Trillions	TB

For Arithmetic Presentation:

8bits = B

100B = HB

1000B = KB

1000KB = MB

1000MB = GB

1000GB = TB

Note that in counting of characters, we can use *'Character with Space'* and *'Character without Space'*. In the other words, space, comma, full-stop, etc. that we may enter during typing of data or file creation are also counted as characters.

INTRODUCTION TO FILE-NAMING CONVENTION

Files in major classifications are sound, characters, and image. By composition, sound files can be audio, and part of image (i.e. if it is in a video format). Beside the sound files are the character files, which comprised numbers, symbols, and alphabets. In addition, are the image files that comprise pictures, and part of sound (i.e. if it is in the video format). At computer programmed default, every computer file is subject to computer file-naming convention.

By file-naming convention, we are referring to a systematic structure, which the process of naming a file must follow in order to be usable. In this aspect, this systematic structure can as well be referring as syntax of naming a file. By syntax, it becomes the set of rules that govern the way of naming a file.

Generally, in every saved or already named file, we have *the filename, the separator*, and *the extension*. For example, the filename *"caplus.pdf"* is a character file bearing the name *'caplus'*, the *'dot(.)'* as the 'separator', and *'pdf'* as the extension.

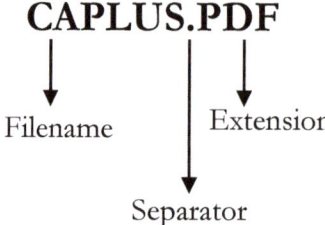

CAPLUS.PDF

Filename Extension

Separator

Meaningful Filename Concept

Meaningful filename is a computer operational way of saving a file with a name related to the content of the file. The purpose is to create easy identification of the file among other files. Although, it is not wrong to save a file with any kind of *able-to-pronounce-word(s)*, or *not-able-to-pronounce-word(s)*, but it is good to use *content-related-name*. So by conventional rule, we are not allowed from computer programs to save a file name with some symbols like * ">"and others. This is because the computer will not be able to recognize them. Although, symbols like currency signs, and arithmetic signs are allowed.

Some characters that cannot be use in file-naming

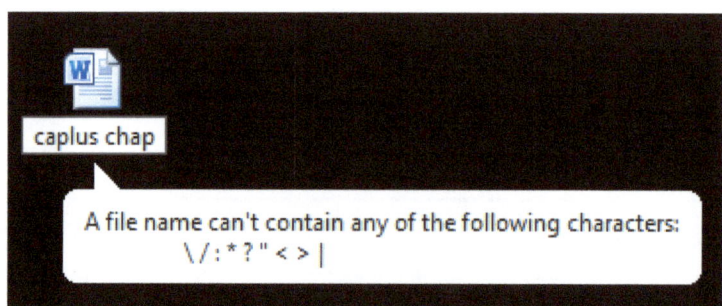

caplus chap

A file name can't contain any of the following characters:
\ / : * ? " < > |

Sample of Invalid filename

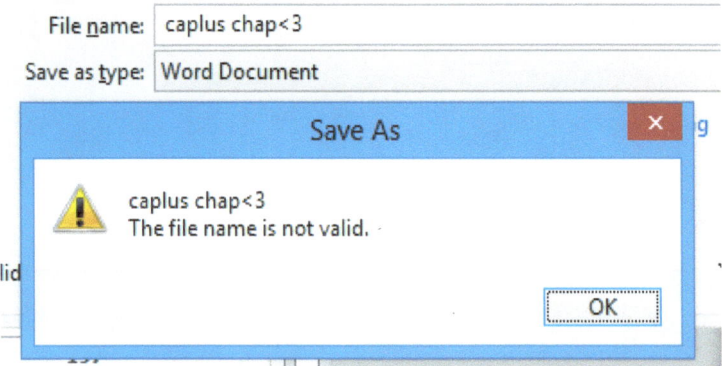

File Extension; PDF and XPS

The extension of a file is the format of that file. By default, files that run in Microcomputers are classified in different formats, which include .pdf, .docx, pptx, xlsx, .xps, jpeg, wma, and others.

Portable Document Format (PDF)

This is a file format used to present documents in a manner where they will be independent of application software, hardware, and operating systems. A file published in this format is characterized with a complete description of a fixed-layout flat document, including the text, fonts, graphics, and other information needed to display it.

In document management, PDF files are very friendly both in reading, printing, and protection of files. For instance, an advance publishing of a file in this format, can prevent unauthorized printing, and content-copying of the file through the process of password encryption. Unless the password is entered or broken, second person cannot print or copy the file content. Moreover, for publication, to publish a document in the PDF or PD Format, we need to save directly in its format, or use any of the third-party software and do the printing or publishing. For examples, a proper configured Microsoft Office 2007 can enable us publish directly in PDF. The 2010 of it (Microsoft Office 2010) can enable us also to publish directly at default. In addition, third-party software like *dopdf* is used to print any form of document into PDF file. (To know more about *dopdf*, visit *www.dopdf.com*)

Historically, been developed by Adobe Systems, it was developed in the early 1990s as a way to share documents, including text formatting and inline images, among computer users of disparate platforms who may not have access to mutually-compatible. Records bear it that in 1991, Adobe Systems co-founder John Warnock outlined a system called "Camelot" that evolved into PDF[1].

Today, the integrity and longevity of more than one billion PDF files in existence is ensured by the ISO 32000 open standard, which is the foundation of special purpose PDF standard, and has enlisted PDF as open standard software.

1. Warnock, J. (1991). "The Camelot Project" (PDF). PlanetPDF

Sample of PDF Document

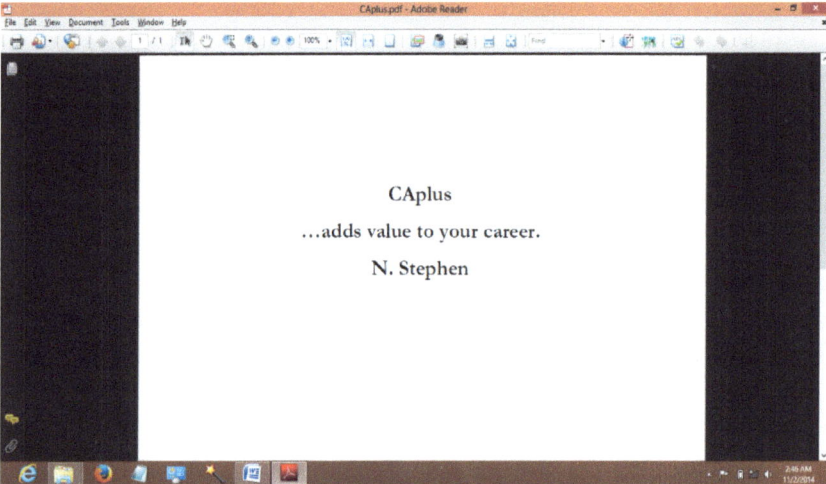

Dopdf website (www.dopdf.com)

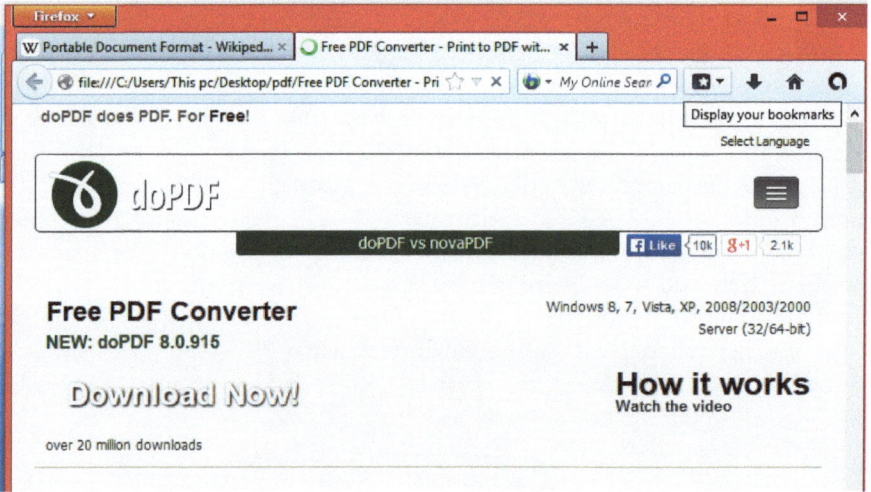

XML Paper Specification (XPS)

The word XML means Extensible Markup Language. It is a flexible text format for creating structured computer documents in machine readable form. Following this, XPS is a document format used in viewing, saving, sharing, digitally signing, and protecting of document's content. Being an electronic sheet of paper, we cannot edit its contents after printing or saving a file in its format. Like PDF, we can create an XPS document in any program, view, sign, and set permissions for its file in an XPS Viewer. But, unlike PDF, it cannot be edit.

In terms of conversion in different file extension, as of when this book was written, XPS documents are in .xps (for Windows 7) and .oxps (for Windows 8) file extensions. There is viewing incompatibility between them, so document viewing between the two extensions will produce an error report. For instance, we cannot view .xps document in .oxps viewer, vice-versa.But, in order to correct in this incompatibility, Microsoft provides two free converters known as *XpsConverter* to convert XPS documents from .xps to. oxps format, and *OxpsConverter* to convert OXPS (open xps) documents from .oxps to .xps format.

Historically, in 2003, Global Graphics was chosen by Microsoft to provide consultancy and proof of concept development services on XPS and worked with the Windows development teams on the specification and reference architecture for the new format.[2] Microsoft submitted the XPS specification to Ecma International.[3] In June 2007 Ecma International Technical Committee 46 (TC46) was set up to develop a standard based on the Open XML Paper Specification (OpenXPS).[4] At the 97th General Assembly held in Budapest, June 16, 2009, Ecma International approved Open XML Paper Specification (OpenXPS) as an Ecma standard (ECMA-388).[5] TC46's members included Hewlet Packard, Autodesk, Toshiba, Xeros, Canon, Microsoft, and others.

Footnotes for this page

2. Global Graphics XPS reference".Redorbit.com. 2006-09-21. Retrieved 2009-12-10

3. Reimer, Jeremy (2007-07-01). "War and PDF: Microsoft submits XPS to standards body". Arstechnica.com. Retrieved 2009-12-10.

4. "TC46 - XML Paper Specification (XPS)". Ecma-international.org. Retrieved 2009-12-10.

5. Steve McGibbon (Microsoft) (2009-06-17). "OpenXPS - OpenXML Paper Specification".

XPS Functionality in Windows

Windows Vista, Windows 7, and Windows 8 all include built-in XPS tools, such as MS XPS Document Writer, and XPS Viewer.

Microsoft XPS Document Writer: Microsoft Windows 8has inbuilt "Microsoft XPS Document Writer" as a virtual printer, which is used in creating XPS document that will be available for views.

XPS Viewer: The included XPS Viewer application allows users to view XPS documents on in Microcomputer.

Common XPS Frequently Ask Questions

How to view an XPS document?

Double-click an XPS document to view it in the XPS Viewer; the document will open in the viewer automatically.

What are the uses of XPS Digital signature, and Permission?

We can verify an XPS document's authenticity with a digital signature and protect a document's contents with permissions.
A digital signature serves two purposes such as enabling us to verify that our XPS document has not been changed after we have signed it. Secondly, it enables us to verify another XPS document publish or sent to us by a trusted person, so we can make sure that the document comes from rightful source.

We can also create permission in order to restrict unauthorized person not to view, copy, print, or digitally sign the document without our permission. We can set time restrictions on permissions, allow as many or as few permissions as we want to other users, and allow different users to have different levels of access.

Sample of XPS Logo

Sample of XPS Document

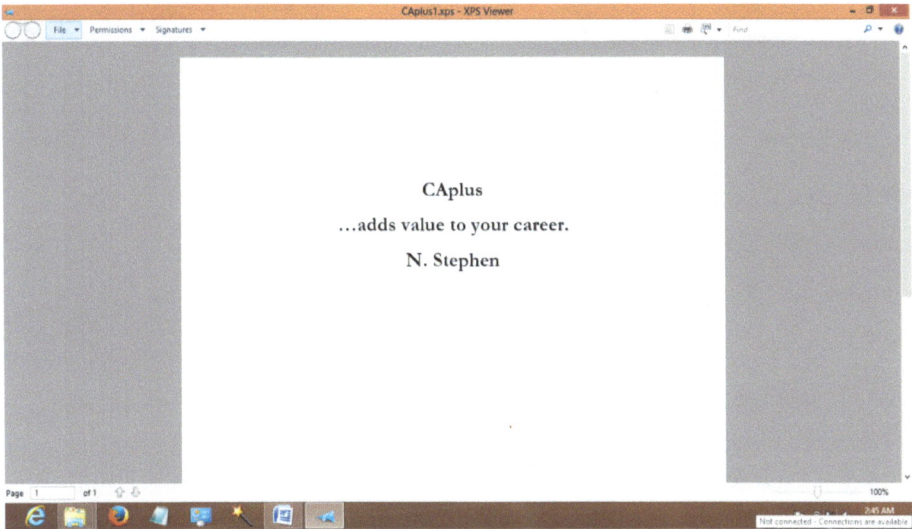

How to Publish and Print in PDF and XPS Document

Publishing a PDF document is the same as saving a file, but no longer with a technical name of 'save', but with a technical name of 'publish'. Although, except documents that fall in the category of Microsoft Office, every other file such picture are to be printed in order to have the PDF view or document. Now printing of a document into a PDF document is of virtual, and does not produce a hardcopy of the document, rather will still convert the document into a PDF document.

Note:

1. By default, Microsoft Office 2010 and its higher version(s) have inbuilt function for PDF and XPS publication.

2. By default, Microsoft Office 2007 does not come with inbuilt function for PDF and XPS publication. So you need to freely download and install an executable file called;

    SaveAsPDFandXPS.exe

3. For lower versions of Microsoft Office like MS Office 2003 and others, we only use third-party software like *dopdf* to convert MS Office document into PDF document.

Publishing MS Word Document into PDF or XPS

For Microsoft Office 2007 Document

1. Install the *"SaveAsPDFandXPS.exe"* executable file,
2. Reboot or restart your computer,
3. Open the file you want to publish,
4. Go to the File ribbon, click "Save As"
5. From the "Save As" dialog box,
6. In the "save as type" menu drop down,
7. Select either PDF or XPS,
8. Click Save, you are done.

For Microsoft Office 2010 Document

1. Open the file you want to publish,
2. Go to the File ribbon, click "Save As"
3. From the "Save As" dialog box,
4. In the "save as type" menu drop down,
5. Select either PDF or XPS,
6. Click Save, you are done.
7. See picture below:

Saving a Microsoft Office 2007 and 2010 Document into PDF or XPS Document

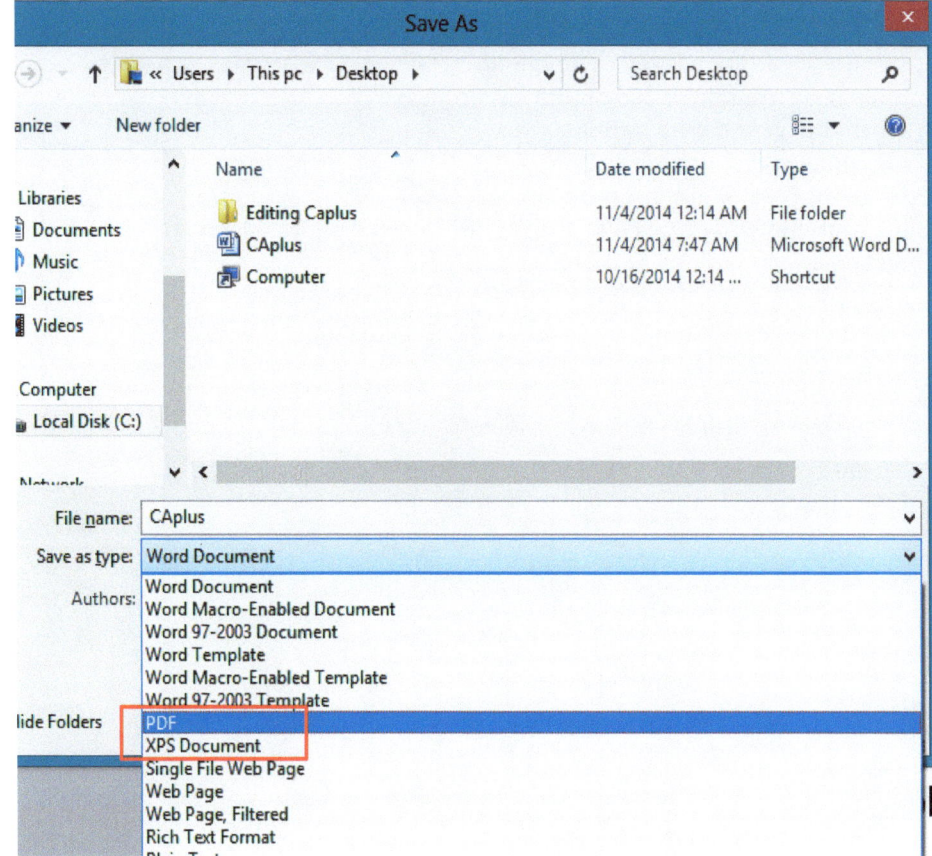

Printing MS Office Document into PDF or XPS Document

For Microsoft Office 2007 and 2010 Document

1. Install the *"dopdf.exe"* executable file, after the free download,
2. Reboot or restart your computer,
3. Open the file you want to print,
4. Go to the File ribbon, click 'Print
5. From the '"Print" dialog box,
6. Set your printer type to; *"Dopdf"* for PDF Document, or "Microsoft XPS Document Writer" for XPS Document,
7. Click print, you are done.

Sample of MS Office 2010 Document

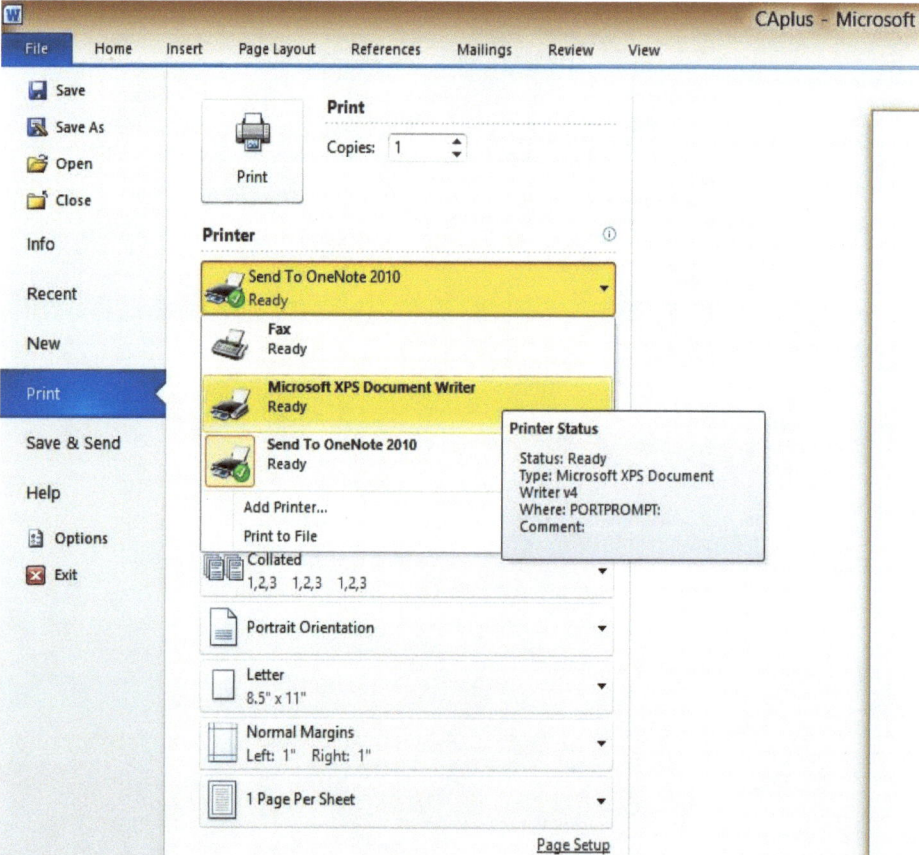

> **Note**: Except in MS Office lower than the 2007 version, there is no need of installing *Dopdf* in MS Office 2007 or 2010, since you can publish both XPS and PDF through the Save As process in 2007 ver. And direct in 2010.

End of Chapter One
Key Terminologies and Meaning

Terms	Meaning
Command Prompt	Command Prompt is a command line interpreter application available in most Windows Operating System.
Control Panel	This is that part of the Microsoft Windows graphical user interface which allows users to view and manipulate basic system settings and controls through applets, such as adding and removing software, controlling user accounts, etc.
Desktop Computers	They are Personal Computers, which varies in both Table and Tower Desktop Computers.
Desktop Environment	This is a location on a personal computer screen, which helps a user to get around and do work on a computer.
File Extension	The extension of a file is the format of that file. By default, files that run in Microcomputers are classified in different formats, which include *.pdf, .docx, pptx, xlsx, .xps, jpeg, wma*, and others.
FTP	FTP stands for File Transfer Protocol, it is mainly used to send and receive files on the Internet.
Internet Protocol (IP)	The Internet Protocol is a set of rules for sending information between computers on the Internet.
MS Office	These are Desktop publishing Application Software of Microsoft corporation Inc. They are MS Word, MS Excel, etc.
PDF	This is a file format used to present documents in a manner where they will independent of application software, hardware, and operating systems.
Windows	This is software interactive platform between a computer user and the computer.
Windows Accessories	These are the application programs, and system tools, which are used in performing some activities of Windows in a computer. They are accessories because they functionally support the works of Windows, and are used by the user.
Windows Environment	This is the manipulation environment of an opened Window.
XPS	This is a flexible text format for creating structured computer documents in machine readable form.

Objectives Assessment of Chapter One

1. Examine yourself whether you perfectly achieved the objectives of this last Chapter, if not, read it again. However, if you have any question regarding to what you have learnt, visit www.onlineworkdata.com.

2. If you are successful, move to the Chapter two;

"Internet Appreciation"

Chapter Two

Internet Appreciation

INTRODUCTION

By Internet appreciation, we are referring to the state of gaining a full knowledge of Internet as a subject in learning. This includes both Intranet, and Extranet. While Intranet exists in a limited environment of the user-organization, extranet exists as Intranet shared with external body, then Internet as a global communication of computers through the use of website, server, Service Providers, and other intrinsic of Internet, which is where this chapter rested its coverage.

So in this learning, the intrinsic of Internet are the basic and essential features that make Internet activities possible. They include Website, Server, Web Browser, HTTP, HTTPS, MODEM, Sign up, Sign In, Sign Out, Login, Log out, Register, Username, Password, Membership, Weblog, Email, Google, Yahoo, Hotmail, Social networks, An Account, Create an Account, WWW, URL, and others. Gaining their understanding will make one an Internet, Intranet, and Extranet user. Though, to provide this benefit to students, the chapter covered them with examples, and demonstration of pictures.

INTERNET APPRECIATION

Apart from the uses of Internet, there are other computer networks like Intranet, and Extranet that run in limited functions when compare to Internet.

Intranet is a private network website that only a few selected computers can have access to; just for the reasons of communication and having access to the organization's information. Therefore, it is been used as internal company websites for staffs to communicate and know about what is happening in the company without letting other people who are not staffs to gain such right. It works the same way as a normal website works, and also has a system administrator, who updates, controls and make it accessible only to the authorized users. In the other hand, Extranet is the same like Intranet, expect that in Extranet, the right to access a website of an Intranet will be extended to few outsider, perhaps another company. For example, under Extranet, a company using Intranet might decide to extend limited user privilege to their selected customers or share web pages with another company. However, both Intranet and Extranet are not Internet.

An Internet is a large group of computers that are connected to each other. In other words, it is a global computer networks that connect available computers together for viewing and sharing of information all over the world. In this manner, any computer configured with the necessary Internet tools, such as Internet Protocol (IP) or Internet Network Connection, and IP-based tools like web browsers will be suitable for Internet browsing.

For usage, internet is used to send information quickly between computers around the world. It has millions of individual, smaller domestic, academic, business, and government networks, which together carry lots of different information and services. It is used to view information on websites, and to participate in Social network. Furthermore, with internet activities like communication, research, learning, financial transaction, marketing, public orientation, and gospel preaching have improved and have global impact in the world today. For instance, internet has made communication very easy despite distance because people or organizations can reach themselves via email, social network, or by means of dropping a reply/comment on a website, which may attracts lots of responds. For research works, data surveying via online data collection has improved, and researching has improved via search engines websites. On the area of learning, there are a number of books, reference books, online tutorials, expert's views and other study oriented material on the internet that can make the learning process very easier. For financial transaction, people can make quick transaction with their banks, and payments, so this has really improved business and banking services. In addition, with internet, people now enjoy real-time updates, which is an act of viewing live-event online. For example, www.livescores.comis a place for real-time updates of football scores. Marketing also has improved because awareness of millions of goods and services are made available through websites both in descriptions and purchasing.

Historically, Internet was created in the United States by the "United States Department of Defense Advanced Research Projects Agency" (known as DARPA). It was first connected in October, 1969.[1]In the other hand, the World Wide Web (WWW) was created at CERN in Switzerland in 1989 by a British (UK) Scientist named Tim Berners-Lee.[2]CERN is a research institute near Geneva, Switzerland. The name stands for Centre Européen de Recherche Nucleaire (European Centre for Nuclear Research), and it was founded in 1954.

1. http://walthowe.com/navnet/history.html
2. http://home.web.cern.ch/topics/birth-web

ACTUAL AND VIRTUAL ACTIVITIES OF INTERNET

The word '**e**' in internet terminology stands for electronic. In internet expression, it is a prefix used as a term to describe offline works of lives as online or virtual works of lives. In other words, it is used to distinguish actual activities from virtual activities.

By actual activities, we are referring to our offline activities (i.e. non-internet activities), such as medical, business, health, learning, and others. For virtual activities (i.e. internet activities), we mean all online activities that we can carry out on internet.

Now, by attaching the word 'e' to any actual activity, such activity will become an internet activity. For example, hand payment made in a place of purchase, say shopping mall, and payment made on internet with a debit or credit card. The hand payment is an offline payment, while the internet payment is called e-payment. So all the activities we carry out in internet are virtual activities, therefore termed as e-activities. This is why we have eBook, email, e-payment, e-registration, e-learning, e-commerce, e-economy, e-friends, et cetera.

INTRINSIC OF INTERNET

These are the basic and essential features that make Internet activities possible. They are website, web browser, web page, server, and others.

Website: A website is a set or group of web pages that are joined together. The group of web pages via website development, design and management often contain information that attract people known as Website Visitors to view at websites with a computer of some kind, including smart phones. The websites are kept on computers called web servers, and are being hosted by website hosting companies. Randomly, there are different types of website; forum, social network, email service providers, search engine, government, business, product, online-working, personal, e-Learning sites, et cetera.

For structure, every website has a "navigation bar", which contains a line of 'Menus' or titled web page 'links' that when any of them get clicked, it will dropdown with list of optional links or it will open the respective web page. Good examples of web page links on a navigation bar are *'Home' page, Contact Us* and *"About-Us"* page, which are common in every organization website.

The *Home page* is always the first page that normally displayed whenever we entered a website address for browsing. It is the web page that will link users known as website visitors to other web pages just by clicking the content displayed 'links'. Moreover, below are few types of websites:

- **Weblog** known as blog is a website that is like a functioning electronic diary or journal where people can post information that can attract readers. For example, most people can create a blog and then write on it with information that can attract website or weblog visitors. Such people who create blogs are called Bloggers. For instance, when a blogger wrote on a blog, the writing will be in the form of a post, which is a single piece of writing on the blog, and posts often include links to other websites. Moreover, Weblogs can have one or more writers. If they have more than one writer, they are often called community blogs, team blogs, or group blogs. Finally, most platforms where we can create free weblog are **www.wordpress.com** owns by WordPress Company, and **www.blogger.com** owns by Google Incorporate. A good example of a weblog designed in Google weblog platform site is **http://nwankwostephen.blogspot.com**.

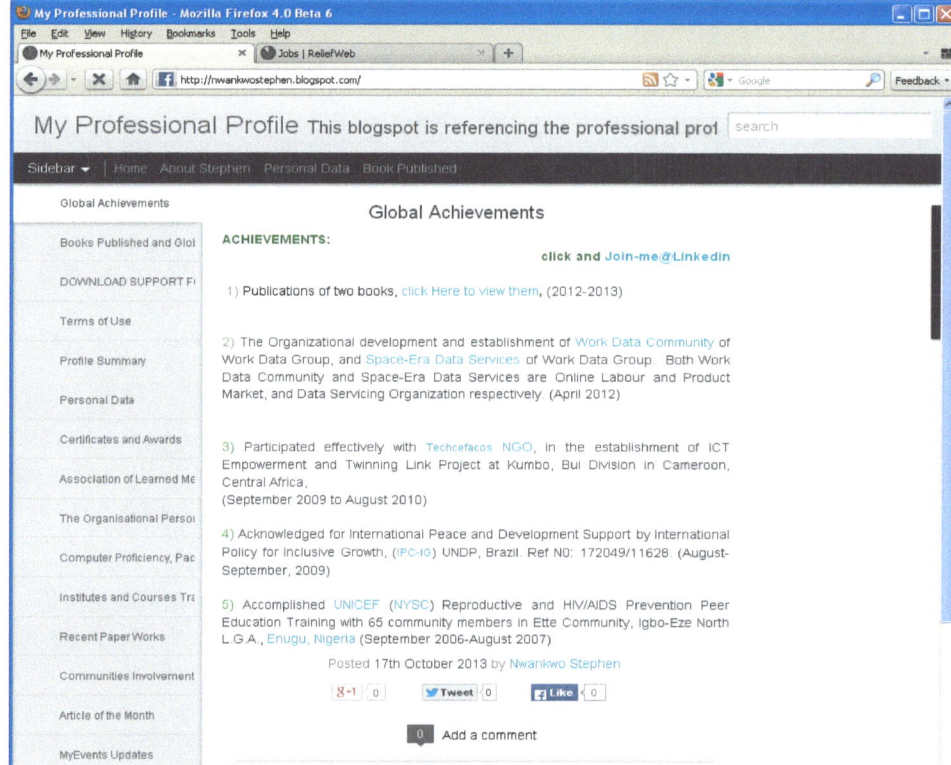

- **Wiki** is a website that anyone can edit its pages. An example is **www.wikipedia.org**, which is also an online encyclopedia website.

- **Search engine** is a website mainly for the searching of information Online. They are normally own by companies, not individuals. Examples are **www.google.com**, owns by Google Inc. **www.ask.com** owns by InterActiveCorp, and **www.bing.com** owns by Microsoft Corporation.

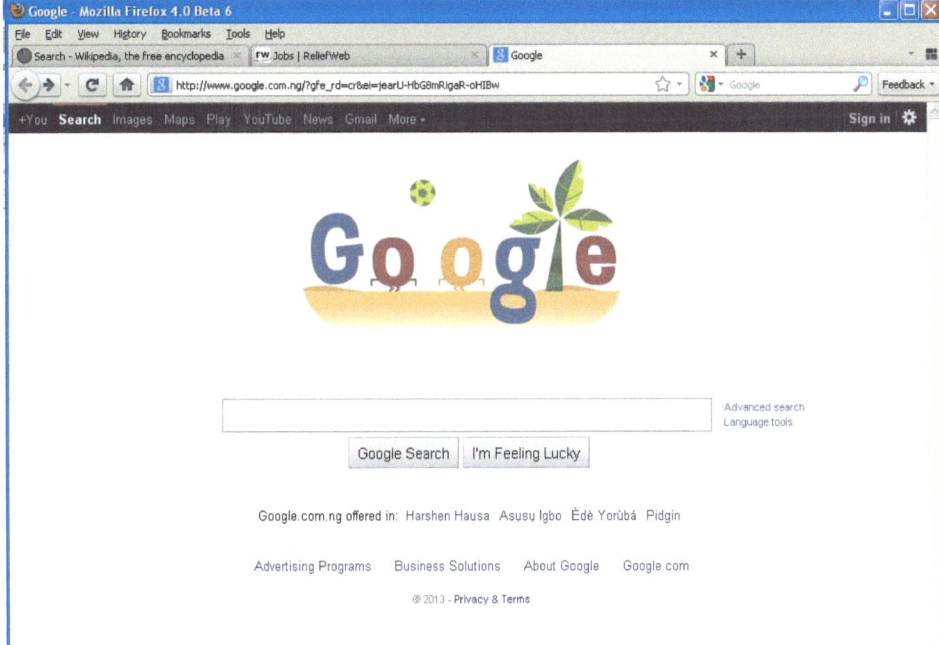

- **Social networking** is a website that allows people to participate as community members, and socialize or relate with friends irrespective of their different residing locations. A good example is **www.facebook.com**

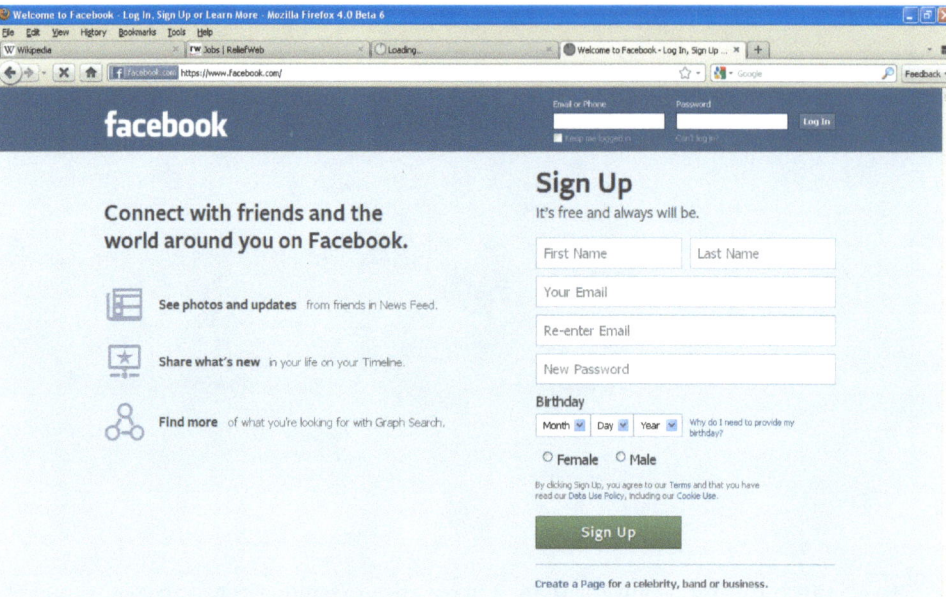

- **Forum** is a website that allows people to participate as community members, irrespective of their different locations in the discussion of some approved topics, may be jobs, education, or package. A good Example is **http://www.App-XL.com/forums**, which is a place to share view of App-XL package.

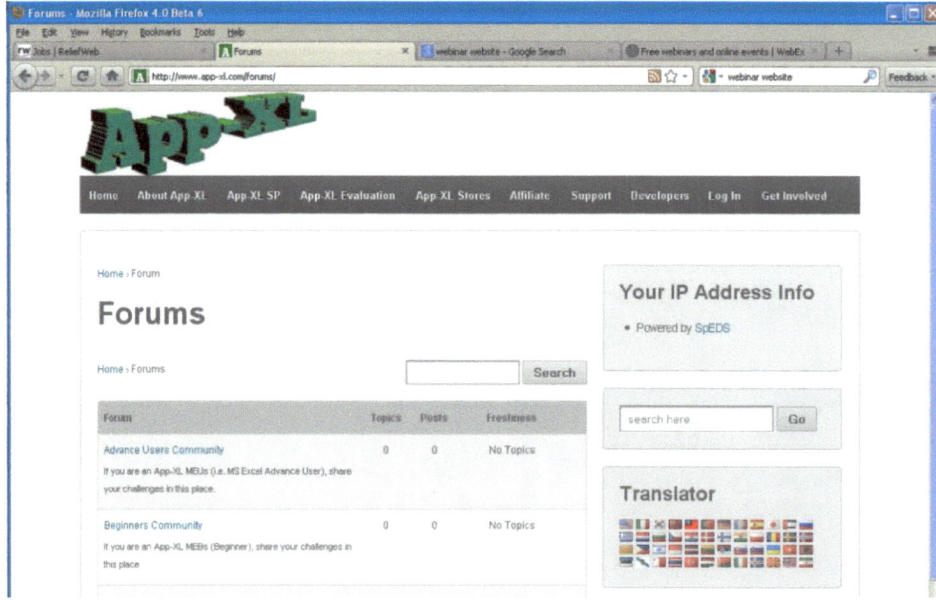

- **E-Learning** is a website, which allows people to study courses online. They can be of professional body or an academic website owned by an Institute. An Example is **http://www.globalhealthlearning.org.**

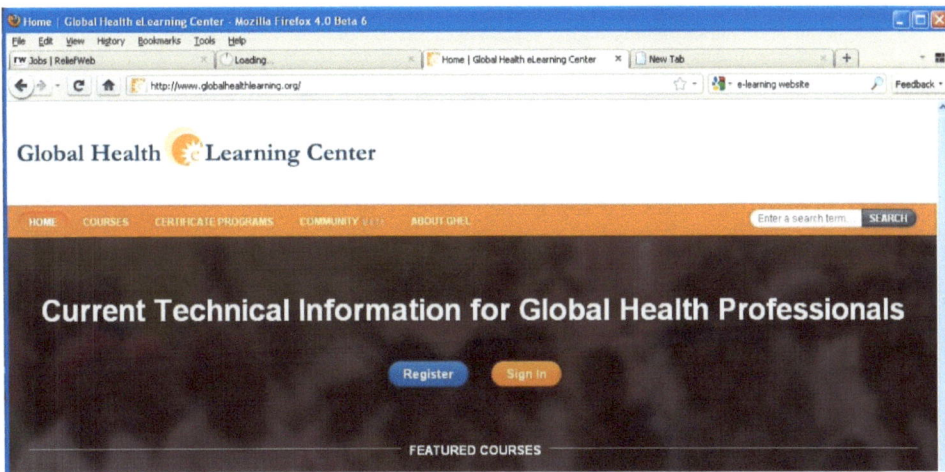

- **Webinar** is a website that permits registered members to participate for seminars online. Example is **http://www.webex.com/webinars**

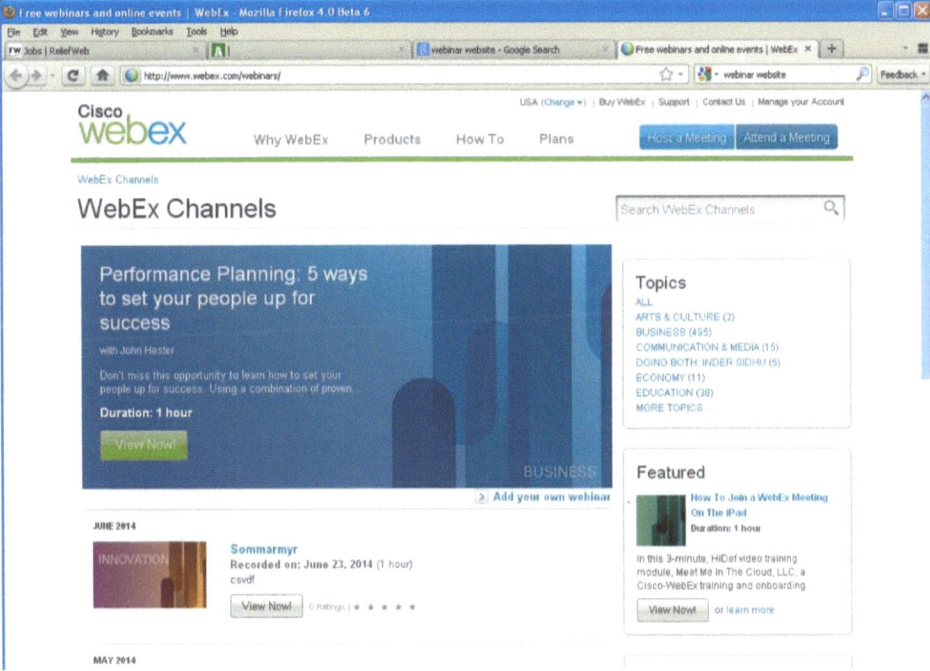

- **Special Information website** is a website developed to display specified information to the general public. For instance government, company, private individual, and product website. Examples are USA Official Government website, and Package website of App-XL.

Example, an official website of USA Government: **www.usa.gov**

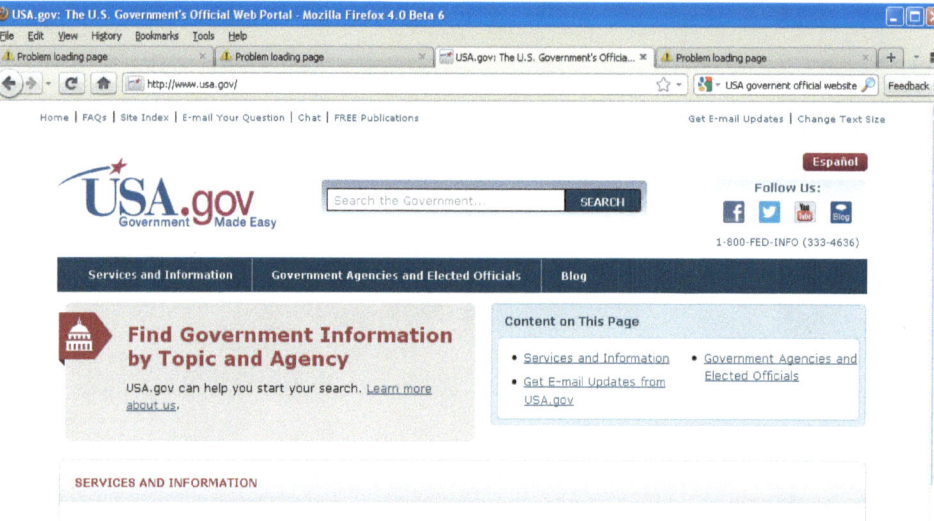

Example, a package website of App-XL: **www.App-XL.com**

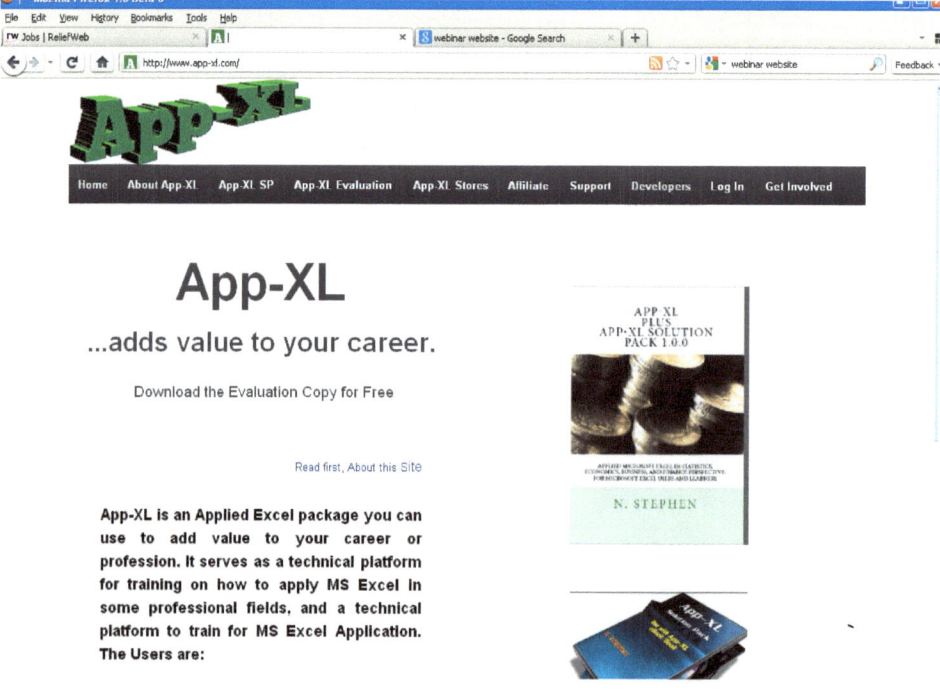

Domain name: This is a human-readable website address that we normally entered whenever we are to open a website. Good examples are **Facebook.com,** and **App-XL.com**. Every domain name has an extension that normally ends in three letters. For example, **Facebook.com** has '**.com**' as extension of its domain name. Other common extensions are **.net, .int, .biz, .org, .info,** and **.gov,** which stand for **network, international, business, organization, information,** and **government** respectively. In addition, a domain name cannot be share by two websites as the rule is one domain name, one website.

URL: This stands for *Uniform Resource Locator*. It is another name for a website address, but different from a domain name. This is because it contains several parts such as **http** and **www** including a domain name.

The HTTP (HyperText Transfer Protocol) is a communication protocol that website used in sending and receiving webpages and files from webserver to the internet. It works by using a user agent, which could be a web browser in connecting to the server. The server must be located, using URL that always contained **http://** at the beginning of its address, and normally connects to **port 80** on a computer. But, for internet security whereby people's information must be protected against theft; a secured version of HTTP is called **HTTPS**, where the '*S*' stands for '*Secured*'. For instance, URL containing **https://** has the feature of encrypting all that are to be send and receive, therefore prevents malicious users such as hackers from stealing its information content or the website itself from the server. This is actually the case on almost all payment websites (i.e. websites that receive online payment), and email service provider websites. Moreover, as mentioned before, HTTP was developed by a British Scientist named Tim Berners-Lee who created www (World Wide Web) at CERN in Switzerland in 1989.

Now in the activity to view a website, we will type the website address or name on the *"address bar"* of the web browser. Take for instance of these websites;

http://www.App-XL.com

http://www.onlineworkdata.com

However, if we type only the domain name, for instance App-XL.com, the website will still open because every active domain name is in the configuration of http or https based on the package or host plan of that domain name.

Web browser: A web browser is application software or program, which when installed in a computer, and connects the computer to an internet, it will allow people to browse websites, read web pages, and participate in the website as visitors or members.

For displaying of data, information displays in websites are read by web browsers in HTML (HyperText Markup Language), which is a language used in creating web pages. To display a website on web browser, we must enter the name of the website into the "address tool bar" of the web browser. Examples of web browsers are Camino, Internet Explorer, Mozilla Firefox, Netscape Navigator, Opera mini, Safari, and Google chrome.

For a better understanding, the picture below shows a Mozilla Firefox web browser with a URL of **"http://www.App-XL.com"** on the Address bar. The plus (+) button located after the **"New Tab"** rectangular box is used to create a new tab for a website. For instance, to open a new website while the **http://www.App-XL.com** remains open, the user has to click on the plus button, then a new tab will open with a new Address bar.

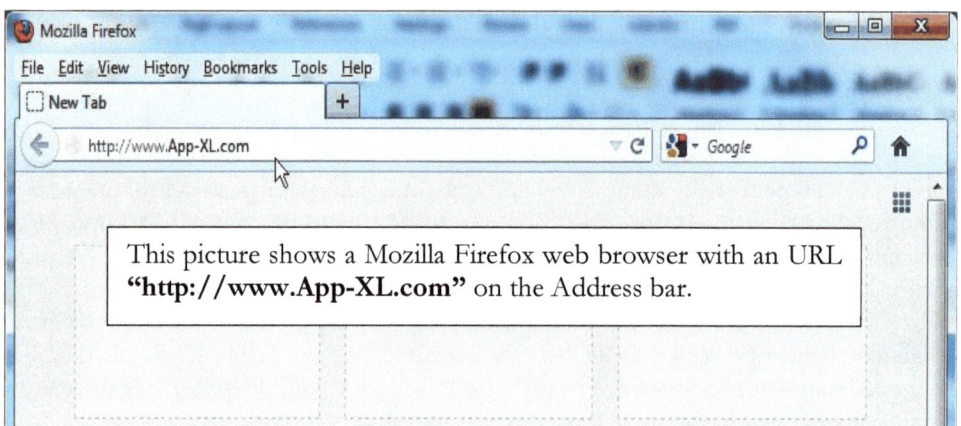

This picture shows a Mozilla Firefox web browser with an URL **"http://www.App-XL.com"** on the Address bar.

MODEM: This stands for Modulator-Demodulator. It is a piece of computer hardware used in communicating between distant computers. In this manner, a MODEM plugged in a computer is required to establish connection whereby it will send and receive data to and fro. In the process of the data transferring, there will be experiences of two different forms of processes, which are the process of modulation, and the process of demodulation. The *process of modulation* changes digital data in the personal computer to analog data so that it can be send and receive by the telephone network receiver, then the *process of demodulation* will change the analog data that is received over the telephone lines to digital data, which are to be use by the computer. Moreover, the data sent and received are measured and charged in bits per second by the telephone network providers.

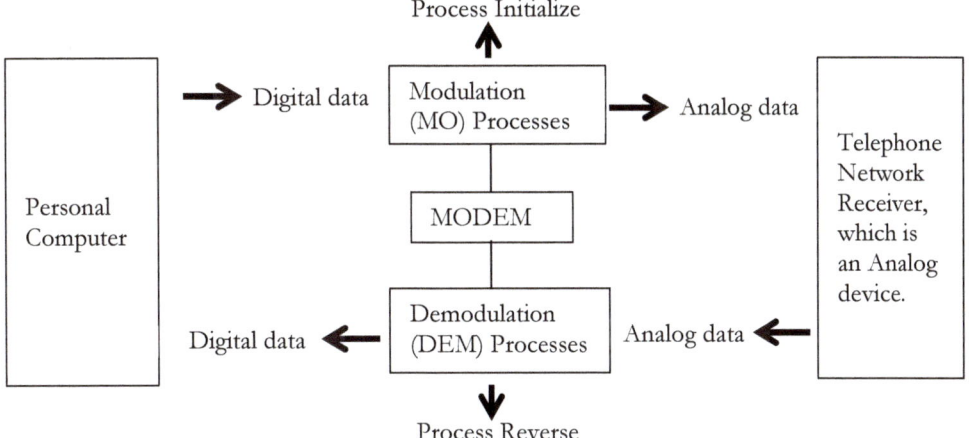

Although, there are types of MODEM such as internal, external, and PC card Modem, but through the use of mobile SIM (Subscriber Identity Module) card in telephone services, they are used to connect Internet services to computer. A user only needs to insert a SIM card on a PC card Modem, plug the Modem into the computer, and connect to Internet. But, the Internet Service provider will charge the user based bits per second. Most of these Internet services providers are telephone services network providers located in different countries.

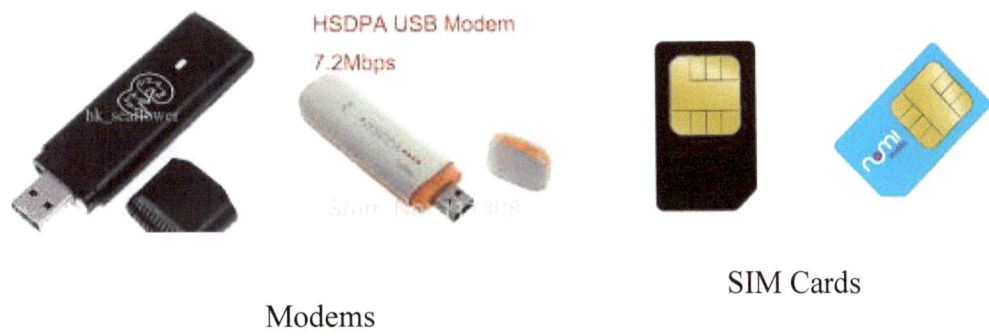

Modems   SIM Cards

Email Service Providers: The email stands for electronic mails. It is an Internet service that allows people who have an e-mail address (i.e. email accounts) to send and receive electronic letters. It is the same like postal letters, but has a faster delivering system than postal letters, irrespective of distance. There are many companies located in the different parts of the world, which are providing email services today for us. Good examples are Google Inc., Yahoo, and Microsoft Corporation. These companies provide an email websites that contain a large database for people to register and run email accounts on their websites. Examples of their email services links are**www.gmail.com** owns by Google Inc., **www.yahoomail.com** owns by Yahoo, and **www.outlook.com** (formerly known as **www.hotmail.com**) owns by Microsoft Corporation.

For the account running condition, opening of an email account is free. One who wants to open an email needs to open any of the email service providers' website and create a free account. For instance to open an account at Yahoo, we will enter the Yahoo email website, which is **www.yahoomail.com**, click *"Create Account"*, fill the **Form,** and get it submitted.

Although, in filling the **Form**, we will take an email address, which for example may be **caplus@yahoo.com**. Although, one unique character about an email address is that two people cannot use the same of it. For instance, during the registration process, if we choose an email someone is using, the website will report that to be "unavailable". But if nobody is using the email address, then the report will be "Available", thereby giving us the sole right of ownership of the email address in all over the World.

Below are browsing terms, we may see on email, forum and social networking websites.

Terms	Meaning
Compose email	When we **Sign in** into an email website, the **Compose email** is an environment to write a letter and send that letter to the Recipient(s).
Draft box	When we **Sign in** into an email website, the **Draft** is an environment where letters we drafted for future sending are kept.
Inbox	When we **Sign in** into an email website, the **Inbox** is an environment the letters we received from other people is kept.
Outbox	It keeps every mail we sent out, but not yet received by the receiver.
Sent box	When we **Sign** in into an email website, the **Sent** is an environment the letters we have sent to other people are kept, if they received them.
Sign in	The same with **Login**. By Login, a **Login** or **Sign in member** of a website will be required to enter his/her **Username** and **Password** in order to access the website. For instance, if you register or sign up in any website, to access that website, you are demanded to **Login** or **Sign in** with your **Username** and **Password**. This is case of Facebook.com and every email website. For example, all Facebook account holders must login before posting their comments in the website.
Sign out	The same with **Log out**. By **Log out**, a **Sign in** member of a website will be required to close and leave the website in order to make his or login webpage invisible to others. For instance, if you login into a website, to close and leave that website, you are demanded to **Log out** or **Sign out** by clicking the **Log out** or **Sign out** link located in the website.
Sign up	The same with **Create Account**, or **Register**. It is used in websites where visitors must have an account before they enjoy the content of the website. For example, all Social networking, Email, and Forum websites required users to **Sign up** before making use of the website. By Signing up, the user automatically becomes a member of the website.
Spam box	When we **Sign in** into an email website, the **Spam** is an environment where unsolicited letters are kept. An unsolicited letter is an email we received from somebody we do know, and never give our email address to that person.
Trash box	When we **Sign in** into an email website, the **Trash** is a dustbin place where we dumped unwanted emails.

Username and Password: A **Username** is known as User Initial Identifier (User ID). It is a unique identifier composed of alphabets or alphanumeric characters used as a means of initial identification by the owner as a means to gain access into a computer system or membership website. In a particular website, no two persons can use the same username.

A **Password** in the other hand is a secret word as alphabets or alphanumeric characters that a **Sign in member** must use to gain entry to a website. It is been created by the owner (the sign in member) during the sign up process, and must not be shared or made open to another person. For instance, **Facebook.com** as a membership website requires every login or registered member to login with his or her email as the usernames together with a password. Although, sometimes members do forget their password, but every login website has means of password recovery.

Gmail Account Creation and Sign in

To create a *Gmail account* or sign in into existing account, we are to enter the website address; **www.gmail.com**, and click **"Create an account"** for account creation, or **Sign in** with existing **email account** and **password**.

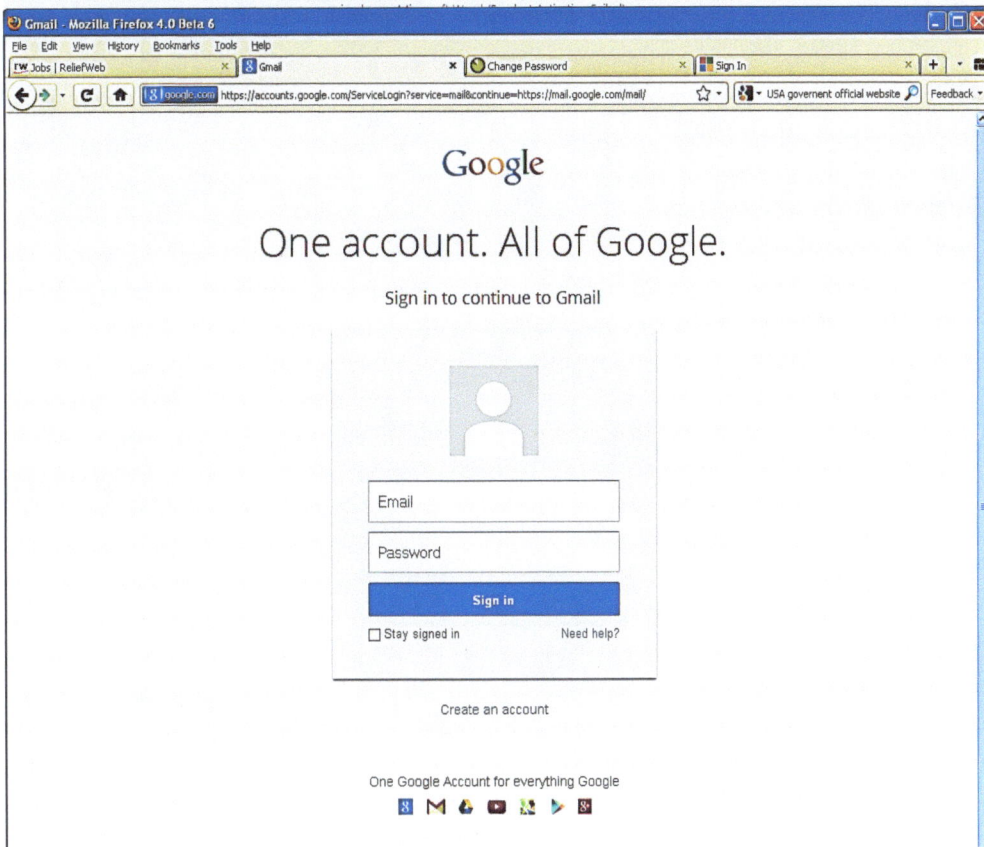

A Sign in Gmail Account

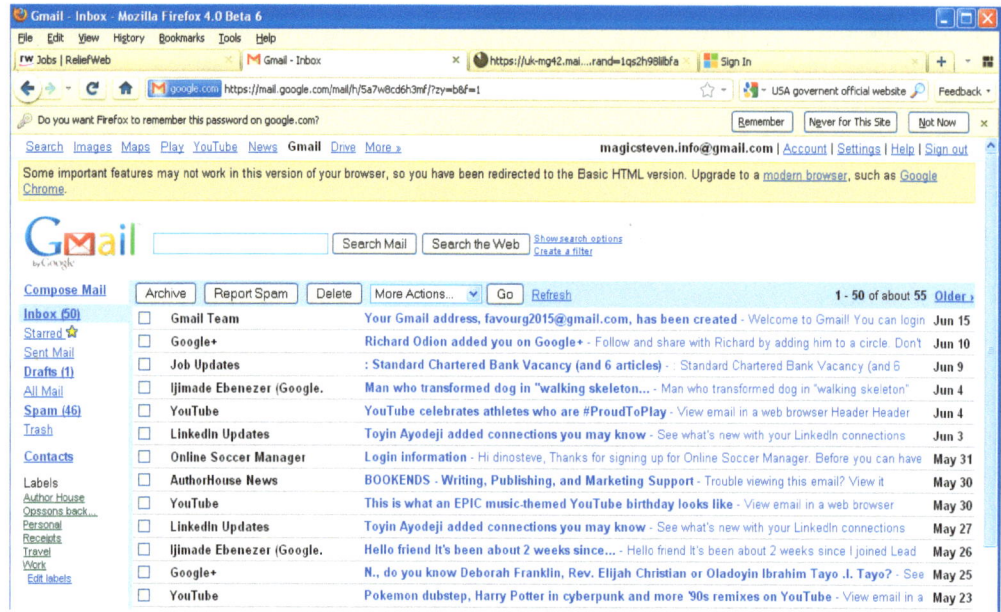

A Compose email of Gmail

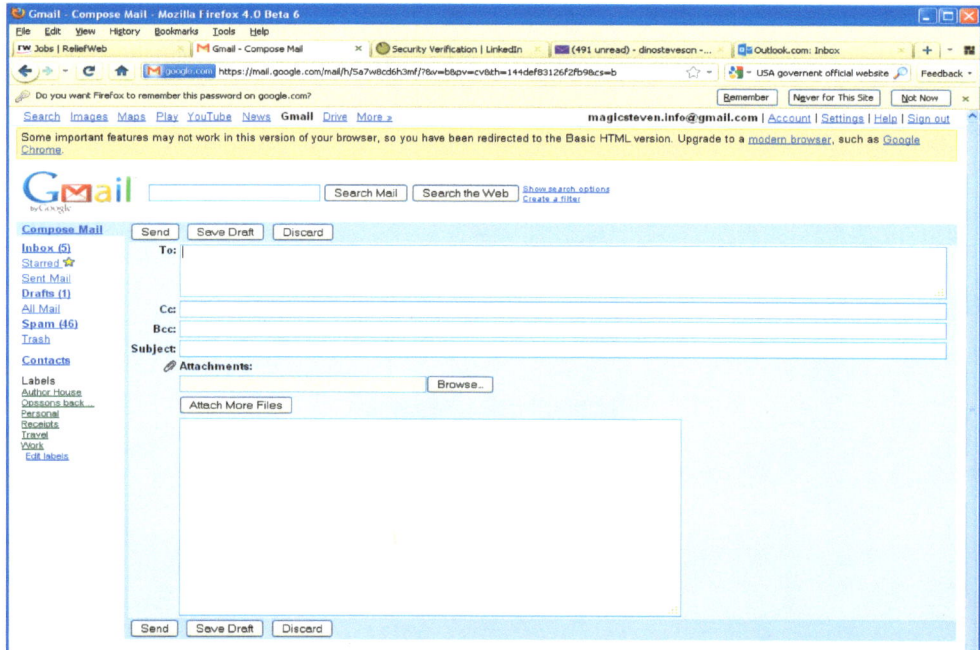

Outlook Account Creation and Sign in

To create an outlook account or sign in into existing account, we are to enter the website address; **www.outlook.com**, and click **"Sign up now"** for account creation, or **Sign in** with existing **email account** and **password.**

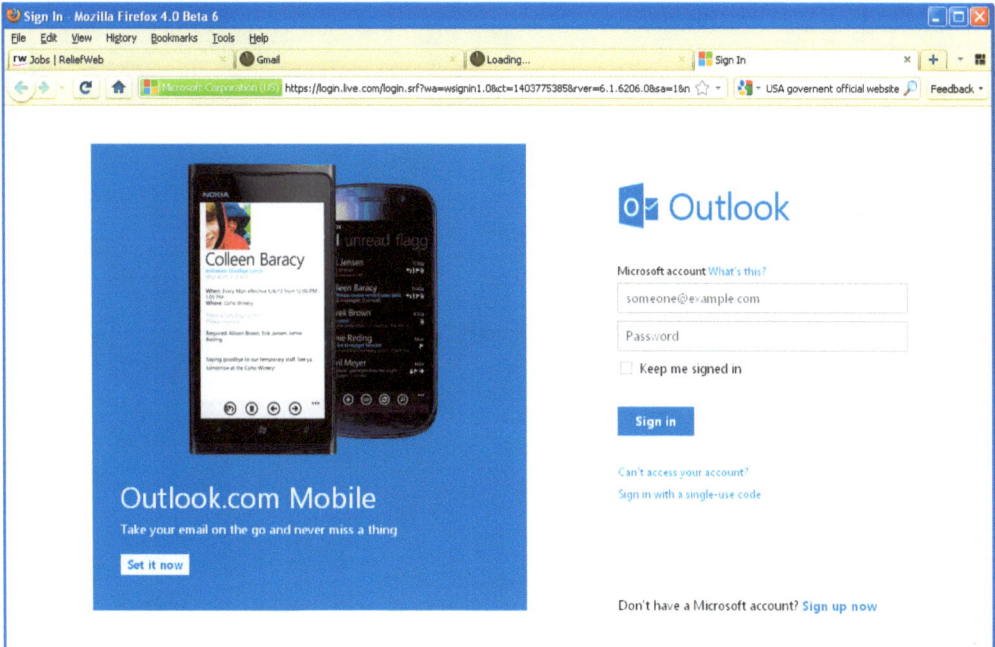

A Sign in Outlook Account, (mobile view)

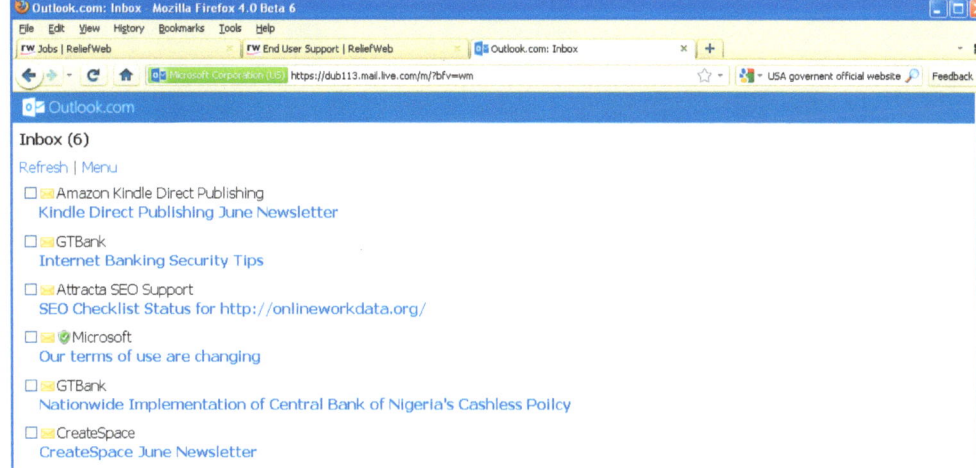

Yahoomail Account Creation and Sign in

To create an Yahoomail account or sign in into existing account, we are to enter the website address; **www.yahoomail.com**, and click **"Create New Account"** for account creation, or **Sign in** with existing **email account** and **password**.

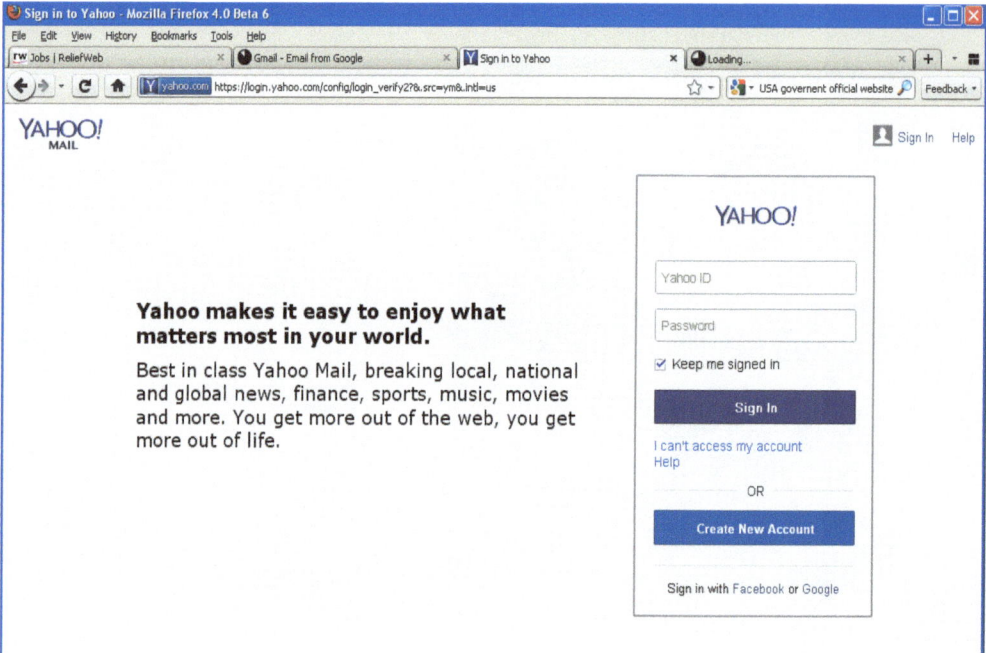

A Sign in Yahoomail Account

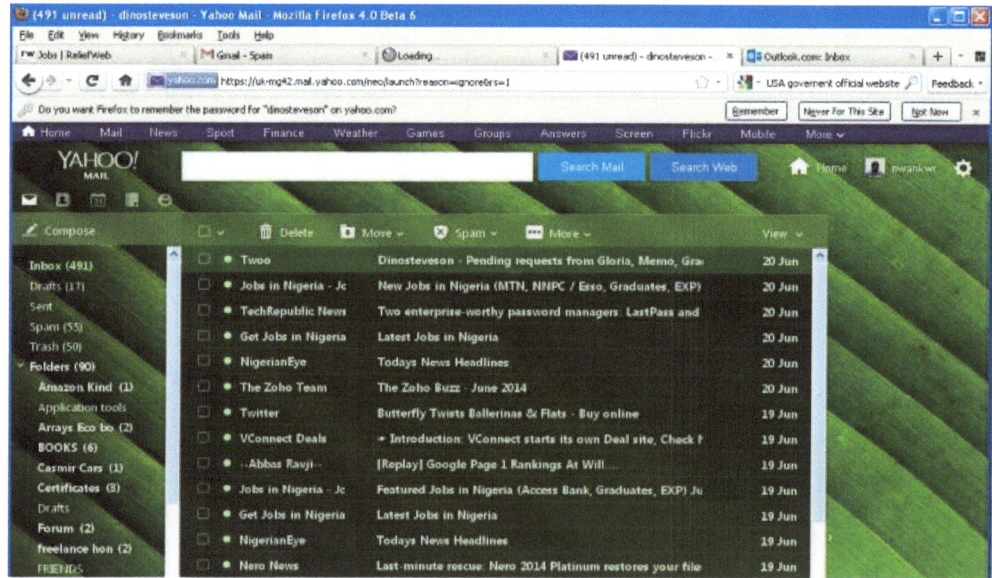

A Compose email of Yahoomail Account

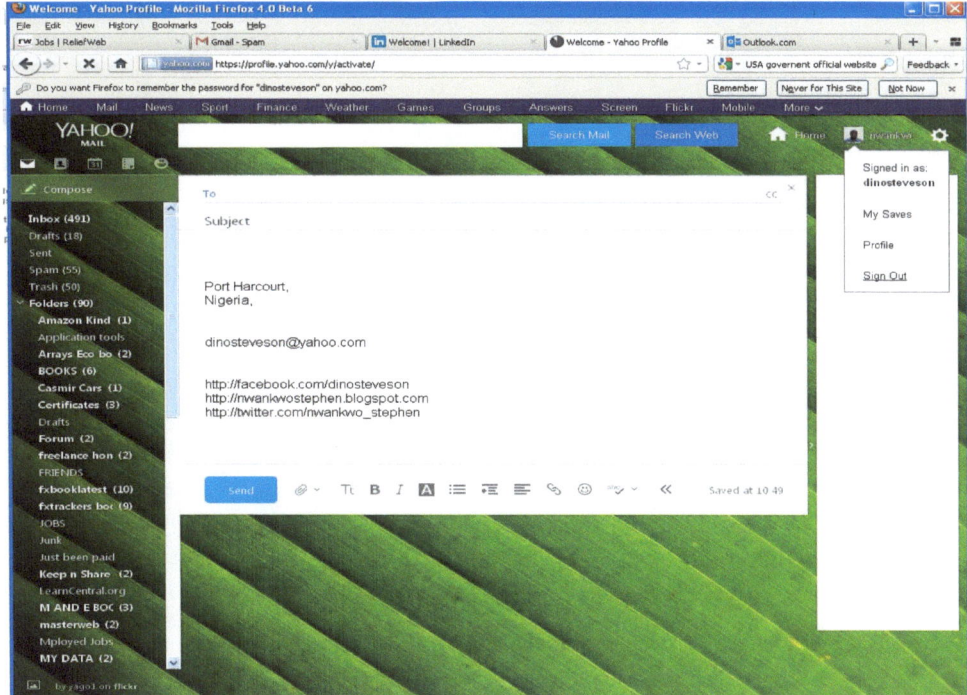

Brief About CAPTCHA

Most times when we will be filling form online or on the process of login into a website where we have accounts, the website will prompt us with a box bearing a text, and asked us to enter the *not-shown-clear written text* or *solve simple maths* in that box. Such box is called 'CAPTCHA'. Now what is CAPTCHA?

The most common CAPTCHA

CAPTCHA from Facebook

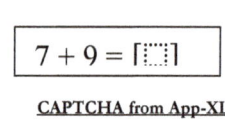

CAPTCHA from App-XL

CAPTCHA is an acronym for *"Completely Automated Public Turing test to tell Computers and Humans Apart"*. It is a program that protects websites against *bots* by generating and grading tests that humans can pass but current computer programs cannot. For example, humans can read distorted text as the one shown below, but current computer programs can't:

The term was coined in 2000[*] by Luis von Ahn, Manuel Blum, Nicholas J. Hopper of Carnegie Mellon University and John Langford of IBM.[#] The most common type of CAPTCHA was first invented by Mark D. Lillibridge, Martin Abadi, Krishna Bharat and Andrei Z. Broder. This CAPTCHA requires that the user type the letters of a distorted image, sometimes with the addition of an obscured sequence of letters or digits that appears on the screen exactly as it is in the screen inside the required typing box.

Reasons of using CAPTCHA

Preventing Comment Spam in Blogs: Most bloggers are familiar with programs that submit bogus comments, usually for the purpose of raising search engine ranks of their website. This is called comment spam. By using a CAPTCHA, only humans can enter comments on a blog. There is no need to make users sign up before they enter a comment.

Protecting Website Registration: Several companies like Yahoo!, Microsoft, and Google offer free email services. For sometime, they suffered attacks from bots registering thousands of email accounts within a given time. So to overcome this challenge, CAPTCHA became the solution to make sure that it is only human being can register in their websites.

Preventing Email Address Harvesting: With Spam-bots (email address harvester software) Spammers crawled websites in search of email addresses posted in clear text. How with CAPTCHA visitors are require to solve CAPTCHA before showing seeing an email address.

Others: CAPTCHA is used in prevent bots from online-pool, dictionary attacks and search engine activity of reading websites.

*. Walsh, Eric (Oct. 28, 2013). "CAPTCHA he cracked by artificial intelligence". mybroadband.co.za. Reuters. Retrieved. Nov. 27 2013
#. Engber, Daniel (Jan. 17, 2014). "Who Made That CAPTCHA". Nytimes.com. NYT. Retrieved January.17, 2014.

End of Chapter Two
Key Terminologies and Meaning

Terms	Meaning
Bloggers	Online article developers whose business is to post articles on weblogs, and welcome comments from the visitors that visit them.
Bots	They are program software that automatically fills forms and registers on websites in other to harvest email addresses and people information. It is used for internet criminal activities.
Compose email	When we **Sign in** into an email website, the **Compose email** is an environment to write a letter and send that letter to the Recipient(s).
Draft box	When we **Sign in** into an email website, the **Draft** is an environment where letters we drafted for future sending are kept.
Inbox	When we **Sign in** into an email website, the **Inbox** keeps all the email we have received from others.
IP	IP stands for Internet Protocol, which is a set of rules for sending information between computers on the Internet. Each computer that uses the IP has at least one IP address that identifies it to all other devices on the planet, just like a person might have a postal address.
IP Address	An IP (Internet Protocol) address is a number given to each computer on the internet. It is like a postal address or telephone number, which defines how communication from one address to another work.
Outbox	When we Sing in, the Outbox keeps all the email we sent, but have not been receive by their receivers.
Sent box	When we **Sign in** into an email website, the **Sent box** keeps all the email we have sent, and have been received by their receivers.
Sign in	The same with **Login**. By Login or **Sign in,** a member of a website will be required to enter his/her **Username** and **Password** in order to access the website. For instance, if you register or sign up in any website, to access that website, you are demanded to **Login** or **Sign in** with your **Username** and **Password**. This is case of Facebook.com and every email website.
Sign out	The same with **Log out**. By **Log out**, a **Sign in** member of a website will be required to close and leave the website in order to make his or login webpage invisible to others. For instance, if you login into a website, to close and leave that website, you are demanded to **Log out** or **Sign out** by clicking the **Log out** or **Sign out** link located in the website.
Sign up	The same with **Create Account**, or **Register**. It is used in websites where visitors must have an account before they enjoy the content of the website. For example, all Social networking, Email, and Forum websites required users to **Sign up** before making use of the website. By Signing up, the user automatically becomes a member of the website.
Spam box	When we **Sign in** into an email website, the **Spam box** is a folder where unsolicited emails are kept. An unsolicited email is an email we received from somebody we did not share our email address with.
Spammers	Those who works is to collect peoples email addresses online without their permission or notice.
Trash box	When we **Sign in** into an email website, the **Trash** is a dustbin place where we dumped unwanted emails.
Web page	A webpage is part of a website. It is in the form of text and images connected by links. Clicking on a link makes another webpage appear. Webpages are hosted on web servers and are viewed with a web browser.

Objectives Assessment of Chapter two

1. Examine yourself whether you perfectly achieved the objectives of this last chapter, if not, read it again. However, if you have any question regarding to what you have learnt, visit www.onlineworkdata.com.

2. If you are successful, move to the next Chapter;

"Computer Threat Appreciation"

INTRODUCTION

By form of executable code, computer threat can spread from one computer to another if its host is taking to a targeted computer. For general classification, these threats include malware in the form of computer viruses, worms, Trojan horses, rootkits, spyware, adware and other malicious and unwanted software. Though, computer viruses are sometimes confused with some malware like worms and Trojan horses, which are technically different. For instance, a worm can exploit security vulnerabilities in order to spread itself automatically to other computers through networks, while a Trojan horse is a program that appears harmless, but hides malicious functions within itself. In the manner of viruses, both of them can harm a computer system's data or performance. As for spreading, a virus requires user intervention to spread, whereas a worm spreads itself automatically. Although, whether malware or virus, "infected users" are destined to experience system damaged or crashed, stolen of confidential information by unknown person or group via Internet usage, and other damages such as files destruction. Truly, how this virus originated has been major concern to computer users, both organizations, government and private individuals, therefore, their discussions cannot be ignore, and ways to combat them are ongoing processes.

So in this Chapter, whenever we mention malware, we are referring to computer viruses, worms, Trojan horses, spyware, adware, rootkits, and other malicious and unwanted software or programs. For the purpose of our learning, we will take a historical review of assumed origin of computer threats, look into the different meaning that people gave it, its nature and type, how to know when a system is infected, how to combat it, and ways to prevent it.

WHAT IS COMPUTER MALWARE

When software is integrated with a virus during its development or through modification by another party, which is not actually the original developer, such software becomes malicious software, which is shortly called malware.

The name malware is common to every PC users, including Internet users. It is malicious software that is of encrypted or program coded. For encrypted code, it is written with an aim to secretly access the information of a computer user without the user consent or authorization. But, as a program code, it is installed or executed in any computing device without the knowledge of the owner, therefore against the owner's wish. Moreover, their prevalence existence is the act of facilitating internet crimes to a very large rate and as well information destruction. For instance, it is fraudsters that create some of the malware, placed them online, and thus used them to gain access secretly to information of Internet users without their knowledge. It is obvious that most of this information include; bank transaction information, ATM card, Master Card information, and as well other information generally.

Adware: Been an advertising-supported program, it is any software package that automatically plays, displays, or downloads advertisements into a computer. It is often designed to follow up any Internet sites user visits and to present advertising pertinent to the types of goods or services featured there. These advertisements can be in the form of a pop-up, which is often designed to appear, whenever an end user uses the associated program or carry out relative activities. The aim of the adware program is to generate revenue for its author, therefore, to achieve this aim, the author may develop freeware (unpaid software) that can serve a specific task, and integrate the software with an adware in order to earn some income. For the level of harmfulness credibility, adware is harmless, but, some of them may come with integrated spyware such as Keyloggers and other information stealing software.

Spyware: This is a threat, which is always been integrated into a software. The purpose of its integration into software is to collect information from the users of the software without their knowledge. It is typically hidden from the user, can be difficult to detect, and mostly found in freeware (i.e. unpaid software). The developers are mostly hackers who are looking for means to be collecting personal information of computer users. In order to achieve this, they will develop a freeware that can perform a specific task and will be in need by computer users, therefore integrate spyware with it. So once a computer user download and install the software, the spyware will be secretly installed into the person's computer. The presence of it (the spyware) will modify the registry of the computer after the installation, and run secretly inside the computer, thereby monitoring the user information, which are stored in the computer, and be releasing the information to the hacker who developed the freeware.

Moreover, apart from stealing information of the user offline, Spyware also steals information online by redirecting web browsing activities, changes computer settings, thus slow the connection speed of the computer, and sends every online activities of the user to the programmer who designed it. They are exactly what hackers are using against financial institutions. Good examples of spyware are Keyloggers, and Trojan Bancus.

Trojan horse: The Trojan horse gets its name from an incident that occurs in Homer's *Iliad (an* epic poem on the Trojan War traditionally attributed to the ancient Greek poet Homer*)*. It similarly to how the Greeks in Homer's poem sent an army of men, hidden in a wooden horse into the city of Troy, in order to secretly get into the wall of the city.

Trojans are known for their trickery because they are harmless, but will expose a computer to all form of malware attack. For how a Trojan operates, it may encode itself into a freeware just to make a computer user downloads and installs its carrier program (the attached software where it is encoded), and once the software is installed into the computer, it will make that computer vulnerable to all forms of malware attacks. For instance, one of the most common ways that spyware and worm are contacted by computers is through Trojan horse. This is because a spyware or worm can take hid into a Trojan horse, which is encoded into desirable software that the user downloads from the Internet freely, and when the user installs the software, the spyware or worm will be installed alongside. But, it does not transmit its infection to other computer because it only goes with software installation, but can be distributed if that software is shared and installed by other computers.

Worm: This is a program that actively transmits itself over a network just to infect other computers. It can copy and multiply itself by using computer networks and security flaws. Worms are more complex than Trojan horse, and usually attack multi-user systems such as UNIX environment and can spread over corporate networks via the circulation of emails. Once multiplied, the copied worms scan the network for further loopholes and flaws in the network. A classic example of a worm is the ILOVEYOU virus.

Rootkits: As we have stated above, all malicious software have virus integrated into them, so rootkits is a code technique included in malicious software in order to enable the maliciousness (i.e. the integrated virus) of the software to be concealed and not detectable during its installation or scanning in a computer. For instance, a malware with rootkit when been installed can prevent the malicious process of the program from being visible in the system's list of processes, or keep its files from being read. In addition, they can have the capability routines to defend themselves against removal, not merely to hide, but to repel any attempts of removing them from the computer. Others can use other techniques, such as renaming the infected file similar to a legitimate or trustworthy file, for example; expl0rer.exe to VS explorer.exe.

WHAT IS COMPUTER VIRUS

One may think of several explanations of what is computer virus. This is because the term 'virus' just like malware is also common, and erroneously used to refer to other types of malware, such as adware and spyware programs that do not have the reproductive ability. So it may not be easy to give an exact definition of it (virus), but alternatively, we shall state its various definitions:

A computer virus is a computer program that can copy itself and infect a computer, (http://en.wikipedia.org/wiki/Talk:Computer_virus).

A computer virus is a computer program with the characteristic feature being able to generate copies of itself, and thereby spread, (www.ibas.com).

It is a program code that is installed or executed on to any computing device without the knowledge of the owner and against the owner's wish (www.ttushsc.edu).

It is a program created specifically to invade into computers and networks with an aim to create havoc on them, (www.infowest.com).

It is a software executable code segment, which is covertly incorporated into the executable program code files (i.e., .EXE, BAT, .SYS, etc.) or data files of a computer or computer network and is activated when the host program is executed. At this point, it serves to prevent piracy, (www.osc.stste.ct.us).

Lastly, but not the least, it is an executable file that replicates itself and executes itself in an unsolicited manner, (www.symantes.com).

From the foregoing definitions, the common characteristic of a computer virus is that it is a written program programmed by programmers during any of their program development. And, this permits a question such as "who creates virus and why?"

WHO CREATES VIRUS AND WHY?

In a near settlement, viruses are born through program code programmed by programmers that are into program development. These programmers in assumptions are mostly Programming students, Programming beginners, Professional programmers, and Explorers that carry out the activities based on interest.

For most students try their programming ability by developing virus during a program creation. Although, one good thing about them is that they do not spread their viruses by themselves, and after sometimes these viruses "die" together with the storage device.

Why doing this? They do this to confirm their ability in programming skill, and as well raise one's self respect among peers. For example*, on November 2, 1988, a computer science student at Cornell University named Robert Morris released software integrated with 'worm' into the Internet. The worm was an experimental self-propagating and replicating computer program that took advantage of flaws in certain e-mail protocols. Due to a mistake in its programming, rather than just sending copies of itself to other computers, this software kept replicating itself on each infected system, filling all the available computer memory. But, before they discovered, the worm had brought about 6,000 computers (one-tenth of the Internet) to a halt.

*. **Sourced from: Cybercrime,** (2011). Encyclopedia Britannica, *Ultimate Reference Suite*. Chicago.

The second group consists of Young programmers who are learning about viruses and for practices and ego, just to see how far they could spread a virus, they programmed viruses and spread them. Though, they are not expert in programming, but have already decided to devote themselves creating and spreading viruses in the name of practice. The major reason to them is that various creations are their hobby, and way of improving their program ability. In addition, they took time to research and find means in which to evade the virus from anti-virus destruction. For example[#], the Creeper virus that was first detected on ARPANET, the forerunner of the Internet, in the early 1970s was an experimental self-replicating program written by Bob Thomas at BBN Technologies in 1971.

The third group is the professional virus developers, which is the most dangerous group. They create and launch so-called "professional" malware such as; computer viruses, computer worms, Trojan horses, rootkits, spyware, adware and other malicious and unwanted software. These viruses in many cases utilizes stealth technology and are polymorphic, so they infect not just files but also boot sectors of drives and sometimes, windows and OS/2 executable files. They can be there stealing a user's personal information including emails, financial transactions and other information, thus sending the information to their creator. Like we stated earlier, majority of these viruses are contacted via freeware application programs, and Internet. The reason is that the creators developed them with aim to fraud computer users. A typical of this group is Hackers (those who access other users' computers without authorization). A good example[*] of a notorious hacker was Kevin Mitnick, who was the first hacker to make the "most wanted list" of the U.S. Federal Bureau of Investigation (FBI). When he was 17 years old, he allegedly broke into the North American Aerospace Defense Command (NORAD) computer in 1981. This was a feat that brought to the fore the gravity of the threat posed by such security breaches.

The explorers make virus for the sake of 'exploration' of the potentials in computer world. They are professional programmers, and better than the third group. They can invent new principles of infecting, hiding, counter-attacking anti-virus, creates new virus construction sets, and new method of incorporating it on OS. Honestly, this group does not intend to launch virus into the world, but the effect of their existence, promotes virus ideas because as soon as the third group hold the new idea, they very quickly implement them into actual viruses. Importantly, they can still contribute immensely in developing of anti-virus software.

Furthermore, one of the general reasons why people developed virus is to fight against program piracy. Many programmers do not want unauthorized duplication of their products, so they attached anti-piracy, which serves as virus in order to prevent an unauthorized use of their programs. So despite the disadvantages of computer virus, it has an advantage of piracy protection. For example[@], among the notable PC virus is a boot sector virus called 'Brain', created in 1986 by the Farooq Alvi Brothers in Lahore, Pakistan, which was reportedly that it was created in order to deterred piracy of the software they had written.

Generally, from the question of "who creates virus and why?" We can include that many people create viruses due to one or two reasons as we explained above.

[#]. http://en.wikipedia.org/wiki/Creeper_virus

[*]. **Cybercrime,** (2011). Encyclopedia Britannica, *Ultimate Reference Suite*. Chicago: Encyclopedia Britannica.

[@]. http://en.wikipedia.org/wiki/Lahore,_Pakistan

CLASSIFICATION OF VIRUS

Viruses can be classified based on their characters, and some attributes of computers. For instance, virus 101 is a type of virus, but under the classification of polymorphic viruses. Polymorphic is a programming character of been able to take multiple data types. In this aspect, it (polymorphic) is a behavioural pattern of virus. In the other hand, the attributes of computers include the functional and components pattern of computers. For instance, disk killer is a type of virus, but, it is under the classification of boot viruses. Note that booting is a functional attribute of computers. Recycler is also a type of virus, but it is under the classification of program viruses, and programs are application files or software, which is a component of computers, therefore a component attribute of computers. So they are classified based on their characters, and some attributes of computers.

Boot viruses: The boot sector of a disk bears the startup of the computer OS. The boot functions by loading OS into the computer memory thus get the computer started. Its virus infection is responsible to infect the boot records of the hard disk or floppy disk. The virus can replace the floppy disk or/and hard disk master boot record program, which is responsible in loading the OS into the computer memory, thus load itself into the computer memory. The final way to attack these types of viruses is through system reformatting, (i.e. if other means failed). However, the best way of avoiding them is to ensure that we do not start our computer with an unknown or infected removable disk, such as Flash drive. Examples of this virus are Disk Killer, Polyboot.B, and AntiEXE Michelangelo.

Program Viruses: Program files are application programs or software designed to handle specific task, and many of them are sold as ready-to-use software packages. For any functional execution, the responsible program file will load the expected task into the memory of the computer for that functional execution. Examples include general-purpose spreadsheet and word processing, database, graphic, work-assisting programs, computer operations and facilitating programs. For infection, the program viruses can infect executable program files, such as those with file extensions like **.bin, .com, .exe, .ovl, .drv,** and **.sys**.

For virus transfer, as the programs are loaded into the memory during execution, they will take the virus with them into the computer's memory. The virus becomes active in the memory, propagating and replicating itself thereby infecting files on a disk. Examples are Sunday, Cascade, Creeper, Chernobyl, and Recycler. Moreover, a joint force of boot and program viruses can produce multipartite viruses, which occur when a boot record is infected due to the execution of infected program files, and in reverse, the program files will be infected as the computer is booted. This is because as we stated earlier, when we boot a program virus infected computer, then the virus from the boot record loads in the memory will starts infecting program files on a disk. Examples are Invader, Flip, and Tequila.

Overwrite Viruses: Most times, we experience files in our USB Flash to be encrypted in codes we cannot describe. Overwrite viruses is characterized by the fact that it deletes the information contained in the files that it infects, rendering them partially or totally useless once they have been infected. But, the only way to clean a file infected by an overwrite virus is to delete the file completely, or reformat the infected file, thus losing the original content. Examples of this virus include Trj.Reboot, Trivial.88.D, and Way.

Polymorphic viruses: These are viruses that can encrypt their codes in different ways so that they appear differently in each infection. These viruses are more difficult to detect, they change their codes as they infect a file. For instance, a polymorphic virus left no trace when it infected a file, therefore making itself undetectable. However, some anti-virus software can detect it by decrypting the viruses through the use of emulator. Examples are Chameleon, Involuntary, Stimulate, Cascade, Phoenix, Evil, Proud, and Virus 101.

Macro Viruses: Macro viruses have become common since the mid-1990s. Most of these viruses are written in the scripting languages against Microsoft programs such as Microsoft Word and Microsoft Excel. They spread throughout the Microsoft programs by infecting documents and spreadsheets prepared under the Microsoft programs. In addition, since Macintosh computers uses Microsoft programs, the infections also reached to Mac OS, therefore affect them. For instance, if a file in Microsoft Excel is carrying macro virus, once the user opens the file, the macro virus will be activated, and it will infect the Normal template of the Excel file. A normal template (which is by filename also called normal.dot) is a general purpose file that stores default document formatting settings of a document, and if it is infected, every file open in it will be infected. To help out, Microsoft Offices are designed with optional setting to inform user to 'beware' when opening a document that contain Macro programs. Examples are DMV, and Nuclear.

Network Viruses: These are viruses that copy and multiply themselves by using computer networks and security flaws. A good example of network virus is 'worm', which is a virus program that copies and multiplies itself by using computer networks and security flaws. They are more complex than Trojan horse, and usually attack multi-user systems such as UNIX environments, and can spread over corporate networks through the circulation of emails. For instance, once it infects a computer and got multiplied, the duplicates will scan the network for further loopholes and flaws the network. Example is "iloveyou" virus.

Resident Viruses: Any virus that has access to reside in the computer's memory will gain a reference as resident virus. Most program viruses are resident viruses because they reside in the RAM of the computer in order to attack installed programs. They contain a replication module that is similar to the one that is employed by non-resident viruses. For instance, a resident virus loads the replication module into the computer memory when it is executed, and ensures that this module is executed each time the operating system is called to perform a certain operation, as a result, infects every suitable program that is executed on the computer.

They can be grouped into fast infectors and slow infectors. The fast infectors with their fast infection rate speed are designed to infect as many files as possible, for instance, every potential host file which is accessible. They can infect large number of files at a short period of time. The slow infectors infects on a slow rate spread, and does not easily slow system like the fast infectors, however, resident viruses have the capability to overcome and interrupt all the operations executed by a computer; these include corrupting files and programs that are opened, closed, copied, and renamed files, including other dangerous activities. Examples are Randex, CMJ, Meve, and MrKlunky.

Stealth viruses: These are viruses that play "hard-to-detect" even with a virus detector, such as anti-virus. They applied certain techniques to avoid detection. For instance, during a computer scan, a stealth virus may either redirect the disk head to read another sector instead of the one in which it resides or it may alter the reading of the infected file's size shown in the directory listing. In other way, it trick anti-virus software by intercepting its requests to the operating system, thereby forcing the virus to return an uninfected version of the file to the anti-virus software, so that it seems that the file is 'clean'. Though, some modern anti-virus software had employed various techniques to counter this mechanism of stealth viruses. But, the only completely reliable method to avoid stealth virus is to boot from a medium or removal disk that is known to be clean. Examples are Frodo.4096, Joshi, and Whale.

FAT Viruses: The file allocation table (FAT) is a system used to store files on a computer drive. In the order way, it is the part of a disk used to connect information for the disk, thereby making it vital part of the normal functioning of the computer. For instance, they can prevent users not to have access to certain sections of the disk where they have infected. And if they do by infecting the disk, there may be a loss of information such as individual files or even entire directories. So the only solution to redeem such infected disk is through reformatting.

Autorun Infection: Many computer users even those of experts have not known the existence of this form of virus known as Autorun.inf. This because they do not know that Autorun file can be harmed and turned into Autorun virus.

Truly speaking, Autorun file is not a virus, it is a technology used to automatically start programs or enhanced content (such as video content on a music CD) when a user inserts a CD, another media type, or removal disk type into a computer. Similarly, there is existence of Autorun viruses, which wear the features of Autorun file and behave like Autorun file in order to achieve effective spread of themselves. So Autorun viruses are viruses that use the Autorun feature of Windows to spread themselves on computers. For instance an Autorun infection carrier such as sample-virus.exe can make a copy of the Autorun.inf file to the root or main directory of all the drives on a PC, internal and/or external disks, thus, make the virus runs every time the external disks like USB drives were inserted or every time a user double-click the drives through the Windows Explorer or "My Computer Folder".

One dangerous thing about Autorun viruses is that most anti-viruses cannot detect them, and some that can detect them cannot remove them. For instance, after removal, at re-running of the infected drive, it will come back on the source drive. So the best way to remove them is through manual techniques, which required running the computer in a safe mode environment and, using of the related Command Prompt syntax line operations.

Moreover, for observation, a blogger[#] have declared that a lot of them (Autorun viruses) were first founded on Bolivia, Viet Nam, Ecuador, Pakistan, Philippines, India, Indonesia, Malaysia, Colombia and Mexico. Examples of the viruses are sample-virus.exe, YahLover (which uses scvhost.exe and killer.exe), Bacalid (which uses ctfmon.exe), IMGKULOT, and FAIZAL.JS viruses.

[#].http://compgeekss.blogspot.com/2009/01/removing-autoruninf-virus-viruses-that.html

THE HISTORY OF COMPUTER VIRUS

The history of computer virus is of in different views, but in a brief discussion, there are lots and many opinions on the date of birth of the first computer virus. For sure, there were no viruses on the Babbage machine, but the UNIVAL 1108 and IBM 360/370 already had them, which are "Pervading Animal" and "Christmas tree" viruses respectively. Therefore, the first virus was born in the very beginning of 1970s or even in the end of 1960s, although nobody was calling it "virus" at then,* and the existence continues until these present days. Nevertheless, we will briefly discussed DOS Viruses and Windows Viruses.

Disk Operating System (DOS) Viruses

The Period of 1980s

Among the notable viruses in this period were Brain, Vienna, and Cascade. Those who started using IBM personal computer as far as in mid-80s might still remember the total epidemic of these viruses in 1987-1989. At this time, letters were dropping from the displays of the monitors, crowd of users were rushing towards monitor service people because their computers started playing a hymn called "Yankee Doodle", many thought it to be a hardware problem, but at a time, it becomes clear that it was a virus, not even a single, but in dozens. Therefore, viruses started infecting files; the 'Brain' and bouncing ball of the "Ping-pong" viruses marked the victory of viruses over the boot sector. And also is the stealth virus known as Frodo.4096. To tackle and prevent the situation appeared some antidotes serving like anti-virus software, which marked the beginning of present day anti-virus software companies.

As time went on, viruses multiplied as they conquered countries differently. At this point, the first leading viruses in Western Europe were the aforementioned viruses, which are Brain, Vienna, and Cascade, then followed by file viruses, which appeared later. Although, this was unlike Eastern Europe, were file viruses came first, before the Brain, Vienna, and Cascade. For destructions, these viruses were alike in sense; they try to damage the RAM, stuck to files and sectors, periodically killing files, diskettes and hard disks.

The Period of 1990s

In summer of 1991, there was a plague of another virus known as "Dir 11" virus, and the like of "beast 512" stealth virus that attacked DOS kernel of Disk Operating System (DOS). But, it was very easy to fight these stealth viruses especially when the RAM of the system is cleaned. But, the self-encrypting ones (viruses), sometimes appearing in software packages were more troublesome to fight. This is because to identify and delete them, it was necessary to write special subroutines in order to debug them. So based on this state that nobody paid attention to it, this continues until the new generation of viruses including polymorphic viruses came. The first polymorphic virus was Chameleon followed by Tequila, which caused a worldwide epidemic, expect in Russia, and Phatom1 that later hampered Russia in late 1994.

*.www.studymode.com/essays/history-of-computer-virus-330922.html

Windows Viruses

From the foregoing history, there was no serious virus affecting the Windows environment, until in 1992 when there is an increase in polymorphic virus and virus construction sets that opened a new page in the history of virus-making. Then, in August 1995, the Microsoft Corporation personally celebrated their new release OS called Windows 95, which in January 1996 experienced the first Windows 95 virus known as Macro Virus.

Moreover, the issues of computer virus continued till this present day that it became a big problem for computer world. In a counter attack, there are many hundreds of anti-viruses software to assist in the combat, and it is advisable for one to be on-guard against virus infection, which is the number one enemy of computer users.

SYMPTOMS OF A COMPUTER THREAT

Most times computer users will be observing OS mal-functioning, and in majority of the cases, attentions are misled. It is in rare occasions that virus will be considered, and the means of identifying the case as virus is only by the experts. Although, there are times the case may be as a result of hardware and/or software problems, which may have nothing to do with a computer malware or virus, but the below highlights may be few signs of malware or virus.

- The computer is running slower than usual;
- The computer stops responding, or it locks up frequently;
- The computer restarts on its own every few minutes;
- Some applications on the computer do not work correctly;
- Disks or disk drives are inaccessible;
- Items cannot print correctly;
- Existence of unusual error messages, displaying that a particular file is not found;
- Displays of distorted menus and dialog boxes;
- Observation of double file extension on attached file, such as a .jpg, .vbs, .gif, or .exe;
- An anti-virus program is disabled for no reason and cannot run restart or update;
- An anti-virus program cannot be installed on the computer,
- New icons appear on the desktop that has not been there;
- Some icons are duplicated with empty folders of picture and music;
- Strange sounds or music plays from the speakers unexpectedly;
- A program disappears from the computer even though the user did not remove it.

COMPUTER THREAT PREVENTION

The adage statement of "prevention is better than cure," can be associated to computer and malware as; "prevention is better than removal". It is better to prevent than to remove malware or virus from the computer. This is because malware attack if not noticed early, and get removed can lead to system reformatting and loss of files (if there is no backup), and a reformatted system can never be like its original.

To protect a computer against malware, we look into the two major ways we can get malware into our system, which are through removable disk and internet browsing.

We can transfer malware like that of computer virus from one system to another system by using an infected removable disk used from infected system to a healthy system. Moreover, computer connected online can get worms, Trojan, spyware, adware or any other malware infection through Internet browsing.

Online Prevention

Most people do not like connecting their computers for online activities due to the fear of malware attack. Truly speaking, for online frequency, computer is prone to online attack. So one of the ways we can prevent an online threat is by "Turning On" the computer Firewall.

Firewall is software or hardware that checks information coming from the Internet or a network, and then either blocks it or allows it to pass through to the computer, depending on its settings. In addition, it helps by preventing hackers or malicious software (such as worms) from gaining access into a computer through the network or Internet, and as well help stop a computer from sending malicious software to other computers.

Apart from the use of firewall, we can install and run updated anti-virus software that has the capability of detecting threats, and configuring our program browser such as Firefox, which can harm our computer whenever been opened, i.e. if it is infected. In addition, get the habit of cleaning the history activities we ran in the computer periodically. "Turn on" Windows OS update of the computer, install anti-malware program, for effective running of the OS, and removal of malware respectively.

Offline Prevention

The use of USB Flash Drive (UFD) storage system is the common way of storing and exchanging data among computer users. Currently, it is the major way of getting virus offline because when an infected UFD is used on a clean computer, that computer will be infected, unless there is protecting software in that computer before the infection may not take place. In a reverse manner, if a clean UFD is used on any infected computer, that UFD will be infected, unless there is protecting software in that UFD before the infection may not take place. So to prevent offline infections, we need to install licensed software that will prevent UFD not be able to transfer virus into our computer. Install and run updated anti-virus and malware software that has the capability of detecting threats, scan any ready-to-install software we want to install into our computer, and avoid using suspicious UFD into the computer.

HOW TO PREVENT COMPUTER THREATS

The adage statement of "prevention is better than cure," can be associated to computer and malware as; "prevention is better than removal". It is better to prevent than to remove malware or virus from the computer. This is because malware attack if not noticed early, and get removed can lead to system reformatting and loss of files (if there is no backup), and a reformatted system can never be like original.

To protect a computer against malware, we look into two major ways we can get malware into our system, which are through removable disk and internet browsing.

We can transfer malware like that of computer virus from one system to another system by using an infected removable disk used from infected system to a health system. Moreover, computer connected online can get worms, Trojan, spyware, adware or any other malware infection through Internet browsing.

Online Prevention

Most people do not like connecting their computers to online due to the fear of malware attack. Truly speaking, for online frequent, computer is prone to online attack. So the below steps can be used to prevent an online attack:

1. Turn **'On'** the Computer Firewall via these steps:
    For Windows,
    Click ***Start* > *All Programs***;
    Click ***Accessories***;
    Click ***System tools;***
    Click ***Control panel;***
    Click ***system and security***
    Click ***Windows Firewall;*** on the left pane of the window; click "Turn Windows Firewall on or off"

> Note that a firewall is software or hardware that checks information coming from the Internet or a network, and then either blocks it or allows it to pass through to the computer, depending on its (firewall) settings. In addition, it helps prevent hackers or malicious software (such as worms) from gaining access into a computer through a network or Internet, and as well help stop a computer from sending malicious software to other computers.
>
>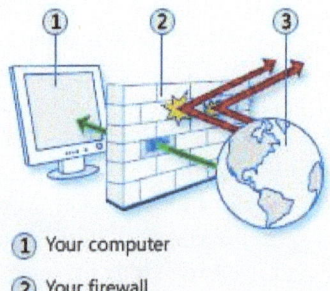
>
> (1) Your computer
> (2) Your firewall
> (3) The Internet

2. Install and run updated anti-virus software that has the capability of detecting threats like spyware, Trojan, worm, virus, adware, and rootkit. And with additional protection like browsing exploits, instant messaging protection, Keyloggers, spam and others. Examples are Smart Security, Avast, AVG, and Norton.

3. Browser Configuration: When browsing online, the risk is that some distrusted addresses or documents could contain malicious content, which, when opened from the browser, and they could potentially harm the computer. To avoid this, it is necessary to configure the browser through the **"Option menu"**. This made it necessary for us to learn how to configure every browser we are using in the style they will play safe with our computer. Examples of browsers are Mozilla Firefox, Internet Explorer, Google Chrome, Flocks, and Opera-Mini. In addition, the general configuration of browsers against malware involves the process of resetting mainly the **Privacy and Security sections** of the browser. For the **Privacy section**, **Content and Clear Browsing Data Setting** need to be performed. For instance, to configure a browser, say Mozilla Firefox;

Click on **Tool Menu box** > **Internet Option**> then configure the setting from the available tools. See below that of a Mozilla Firefox.

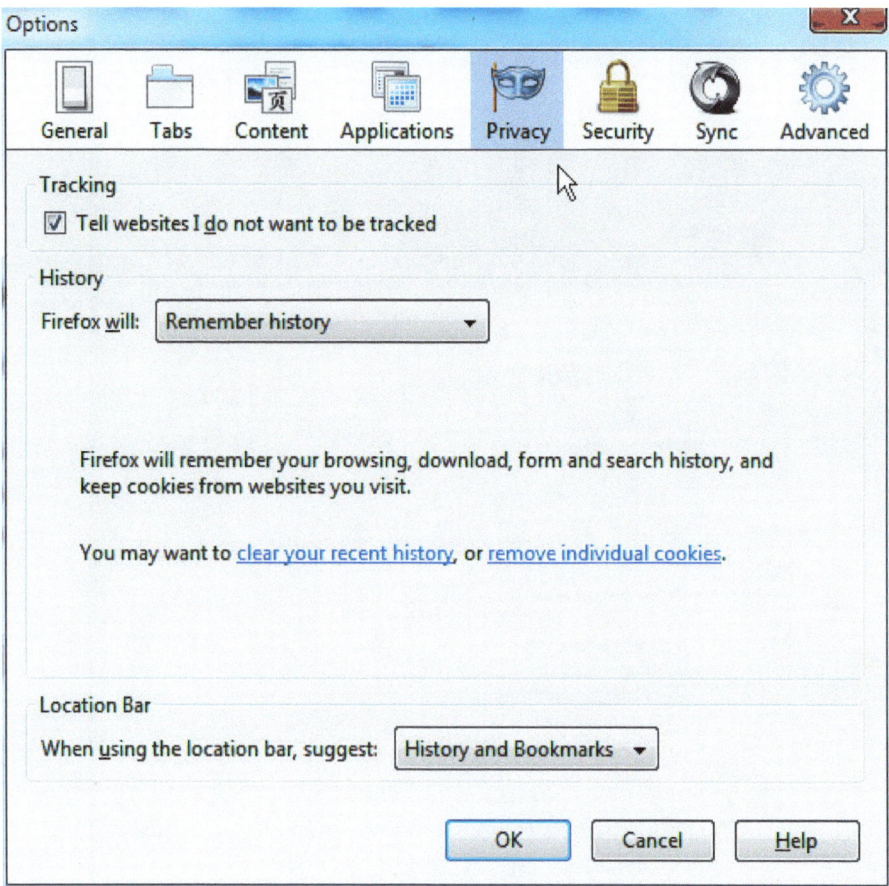

Moreover, it is also good to add the feature of *"Allow Block Content"* setting against *Active-Content* when configuring any browser.

By Active Content, we are referring to interactive or animated content used on websites. The reason is that it includes ActiveX (i.e., technology for creating interactive web content such as credit card transaction, spreadsheet calculation, et cetera) controls and web browser 'add-ons', which are small programs that are used extensively on the Internet. Although, despite its (ActiveX) disadvantage, an ActiveX content can make web browsing more enjoyable by providing toolbars, stock tickers, video, animated content, and more. But, it is good for it to be restricted, especially if a computer does not have strong anti-virus or malware protection software.

But, why does it get restricted in most cases? This is because occasionally they can be malfunctioning or provide a content we do not need. In some cases, they can be used to collect information about us, damage information on our computer, install software without our consent, or allow someone else to control our computer remotely. Given these risks, it is recommended that we only allow the ActiveX Contents of trusted Publishers or Websites.

4. Always use computer cleaner software to clean up the system after browsing, and periodical usage. Example is Ccleaner Software published by Piriform.

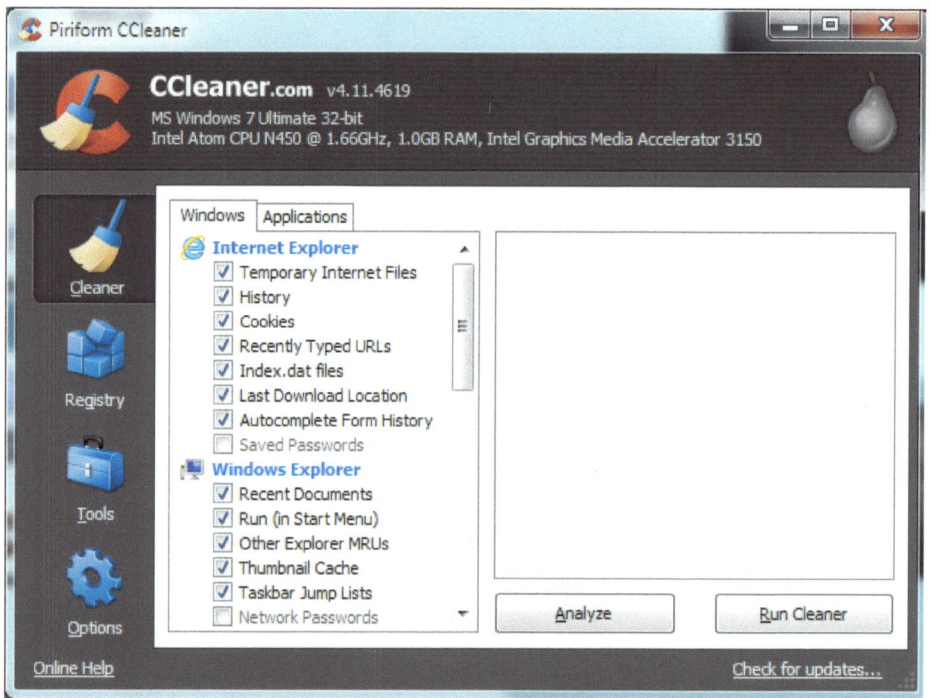

The picture shows Ccleaner, version 4.11.4619 running in a computer named NWANKWOSTEPHEN.

5. If the Windows OS is genuine, turns the Windows Updates 'on', if it is not, turns it 'off'. This is because MS Windows updates may be harmful to a computer, if the Windows OS the computer is running is not genuine.

    For Windows 7, click ***StartUp Menu*** > ***All Programs***;
    Click ***Accessories***, > Click ***System tools;*** > Click ***Control panel;*** >Click ***system and security*** > Click ***Windows Updates;*** on the left pane of the window; click "Change Settings," choose "install updates automatically (recommended)," and select install update time period.

6. Install and run updated of anti-malware software like IObit Malware Fighter. The IObit Malware Fighter work with Advance SystemCare software published by IObit. The software uses auto-scanning to detect and remove malware living in a computer, both during offline and online.

The picture shows an IObit Malware Fighter, version 2.2.1 running in a computer named NWANKWOSTEPHEN.

Offline Prevention

The use of USB Flash Drive (UFD) storage system is the common way of storing and exchanging data among computer users. Currently, it is the major way of getting virus offline because when an infected UFD is used on a clean computer, that computer will be infected, unless there is protecting software in that computer before the infection may not take place. In a reverse manner, if a clean UFD is used on infected computer, that UFD will be infected, unless there is protecting software in that UFD before the infection may not take place. So to prevent offline infections, we adopt these steps:

1. Install licensed USB Disk Security Software. An example is Zbshareware USB Disk security software. This will prevent every infected UFD not infect your computer.

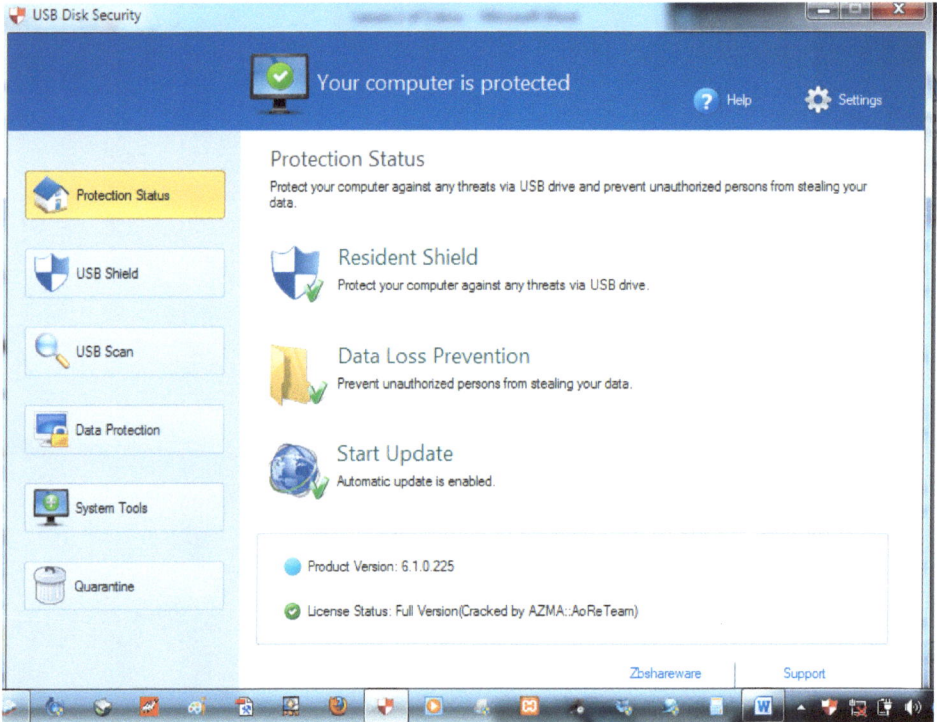

2. Some UFD has built-in anti-virus, so once they are plug into an infected computer, by self-sensitivity, they will automatically go into write-protected mood, therefore resisting writing interaction with the infected computer. An example is Transcend D33193 UFD.

3. Install and run updated anti-virus software that has the capability of detecting threats such as spyware, Trojan, worm, virus, adware, and rootkit. In additional with the capability of protection like browsing exploits, instant messaging protection, Keyloggers, spam and other others. Examples are Eset Smart Security, Avast, AVG, NOD 32, and Avira.

4. Before opening any UFD in a computer, scan it with the computer anti-virus and the USB disk security software for virus status. But, if there is no anti-virus, use the status report of the USB disk security software.

5. Before the installation of any copied software gotten from any source, always scan it, in order to confirm that it is infection-free, before proceeding for the installation.

6. Always scan the computer, perhaps three times per week in order to confirm the health condition of it in terms of virus.

7. Do not accept any UFD that is used from a suspicious computer, especially if the system security level of that computer is not sure. It is better to format the flash before use, i.e. if the stored data has a backup.

8. The installation and running of anti-malware for offline prevention is also good. The IObit Malware Fighter, for instance has the functionality to prevent UFD transferring virus into a computer. It is for both offline and online prevention.

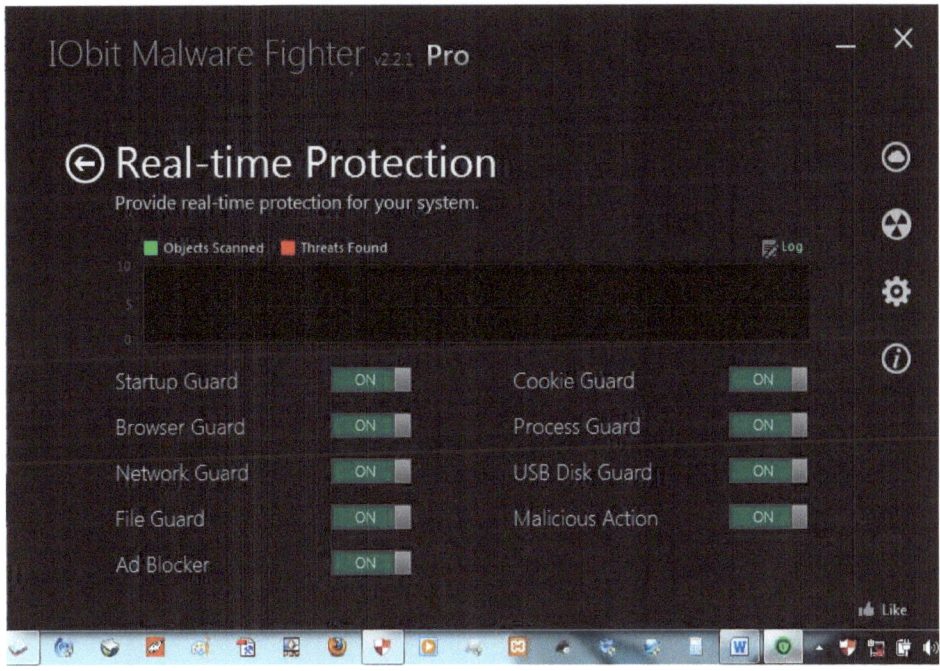

In the picture, activated 'ON' included is the **USB Disk Guard** for Offline prevention. For the Online prevention are **Browser Guard, Cookie Guard**, **Ad Blocker**, and **Network Guard**.

HOW TO REMOVE COMPUTER THREATS

Malware are sensitive like human beings, the moment they occupied a system, if not been noticed early and get removed, they will build fortress on the system. Once a computer is virus fortress established, it will not allow an installation or the update of the existing anti-virus again. So it is good to detect and remove virus early before it will build fortress on the system.

For removal of threat, even for an expert, removing a computer threat can be a difficult task. Some computer viruses or malware such as spyware, even reinstall themselves at a booting, after they have been detected and removed. This is mainly possible, if they are booting virus. Fortunately, by updating the computer and by using some anti-virus tools, computer users can help permanently remove unwanted software or virus. So to remove a computer virus, we can use any of these techniques; use of manual, or use of anti-malware, and anti-virus software.

The use of Manual Technique*

The manual technique is of an advance technique, used only by Experts who know how to work with Command Prompt environment, and also run the computer on a "Safe Mode" environment. The person must know how to explore 'directory' on the command prompt syntax line. For example, an expert in the use of command prompt can explore the directories of the below syntax line and remove the file *"GetMrData.xls"* from the first syntax line. The same method can also be used to remove a *"Trojan horse JS/XUL Cache.A"* bearing the file *'xulcache.jar'* threat from its dwelling root on the second command prompt syntax line, and any threat removed through this method, no matter its resident place in the computer cannot reinstall itself into the system again.

C:\Program Files\IBM\SPSS\DataCollection\6\DDL\Code\General\Excel\GetMrData.xls

C:\Users\NWANKWO
STEPHEN\AppData\Roaming\Mozilla\FireFox\profiles\sz0ye44v.default\extensions\{ab16d209
-7de2-413a-b26f-fda408855dfd}\chrome\xulcache.jar

The use of Anti-Virus Scanning Technique

This involves running an update anti-virus and anti-malware scanning, and allowing them to quarantine suspicious files and software. However, this is not the best technique because most malware or virus like *Autorun* infections, spyware, and others can reinstall themselves after the viruses have been detected and removed. The last solution to remove them is through manual techniques, which is also not the best because of its ineffectiveness in suspicious detection.

The examples of Anti-virus software are BitDefender, Kaspersky, Webroot, AVG, ESET-NOD32, AVIRA, AVAST, and Norton. In the other hand, a good example of anti-malware software is Malwarebytes Anti-Malware (MBAM), and IObit Malware Fighter. But, if both techniques failed, carry out the following steps:

1. Run Google search for article help
2. Back up the newest install software (on the condition that notice of the threats began after few days of installation), perform *System Restore* from the last day preceding the ill day.
3. If all these actions failed; back up all SYSTEM DRIVERS, and all other information in to an external hard disk or large volumes USBs, then reformat the System.

---

*. I applied the listed steps around March 2011, when *Trojan horse JS/XUL Cache.A* infected my computer. I did not reformat the computer rather I used the manual method after my anti-virus (AVG 2011) detected the threat, but failed to move it to the virus chest because the byte size of the threat was too much.

The use of USB Disk Security Software Technique

The USB disk security software like Zbshareware product prevents virus being communicated into a computer and as well delete virus once they are been dictated in a UFD. The licensed version has the functionality of dictating and deleting virus, while the Evaluation (not-licensed) version will only dictate, but will not delete.

For the techniques, once an infected UFD is plug into a computer, the software (USB Disk Security) will prompt its windows open, thereby showing the virus status of the UFD. Depending on the report provided, if there are infections, they will be listed in the manner of a table, and user is to click the 'Delete' or "Delete All" button to remove the virus, and the virus will be quarantine for further actions.

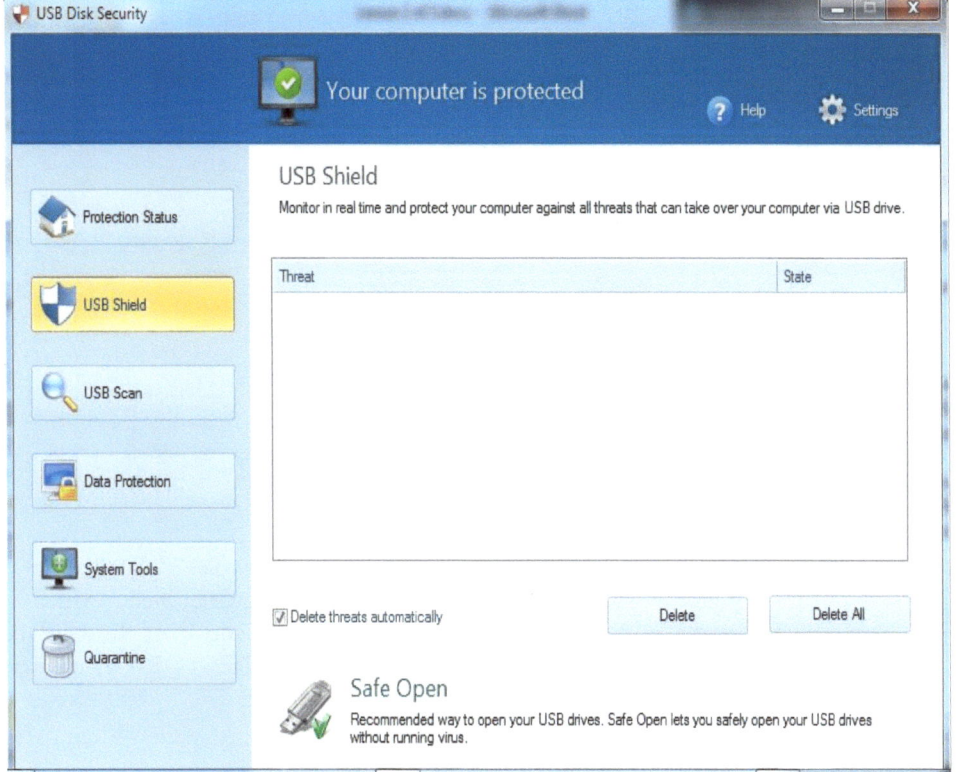

In the picture the,

> **USB Shield:**   Automatically shield the computer from UFD infection.
>
> **USB Scan:**   Scan a plugged UFD for virus status.
>
> **Data Protection:**   Enable/Dis-enable the use of UFD in a computer.
>
> **Quarantine:**   All unsafe files deleted are encrypted and moved in the quarantine directory for further actions.

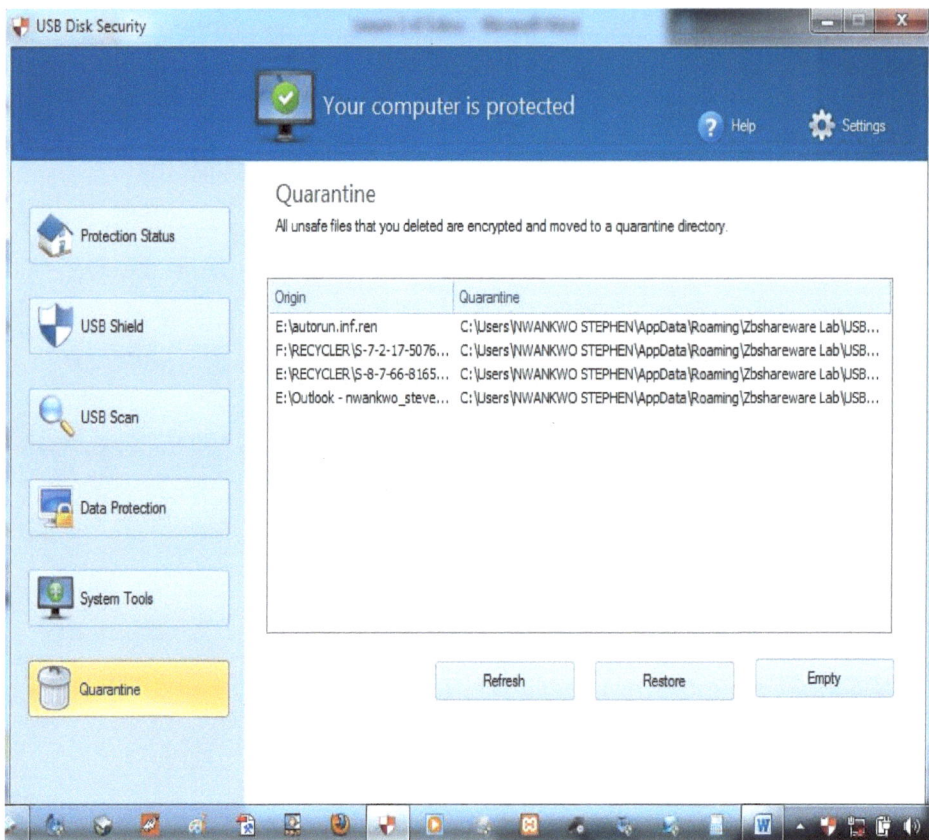

In the picture, shows a Quarantine directory showing unsafe files deleted from the computer named; NWANKWOSTEPHEN. The infections quarantined, which are AUTORUN.INF.REN and RECYCLER were founded in drive F and E of the USB flash used by the owner of the computer. But, for further actions, we can RESTORE them back to their source, or EMPTY them from the quarantine directory.

How to verify/remove Autorun or Recycler

The first assignment is to verify whether any of the viruses is actually in the system via these steps:

1. Open C-Prompt (Command Prompt), may be through the '**Run**' command box located in your start menu, and type '**cmd**' and click 'Ok'. See below:

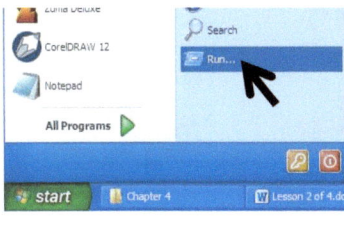
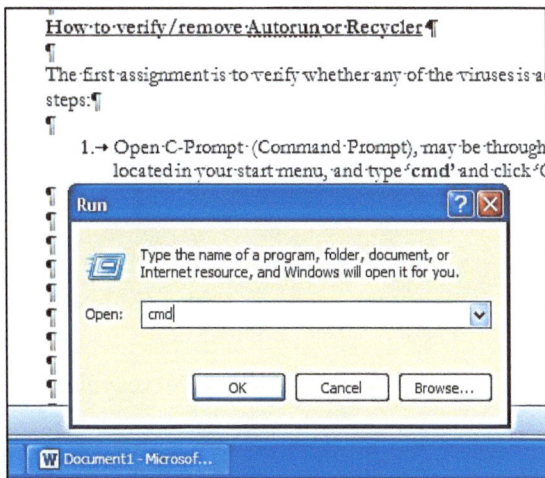

2. Inside the C-Prompt environment, **type** the following lines of commands, and make sure that you press the Enter-key located your keyboard as you type any of the command.

cd

dir

These first lines are for learning purpose, and viewing of your Root folders. It is true that most of these viruses exist as hidden files. So on your screen; there will be nothing like **Recycler** or **Autorun virus** displayed by the computer. But, you can view all the first-directory folders of you C-drive (i.e. Local Disk). However, assuming you are to remove or delete a RECYCLER, the next step:

3. Like the first command, 'type' the below command on the C-Prompt, and make sure that you press the Enter-key located your keyboard as you type any of the command.

attrib –h –r –s recycler

dir

For example, look on the screen as the command unhides it (**RECYCLER**)

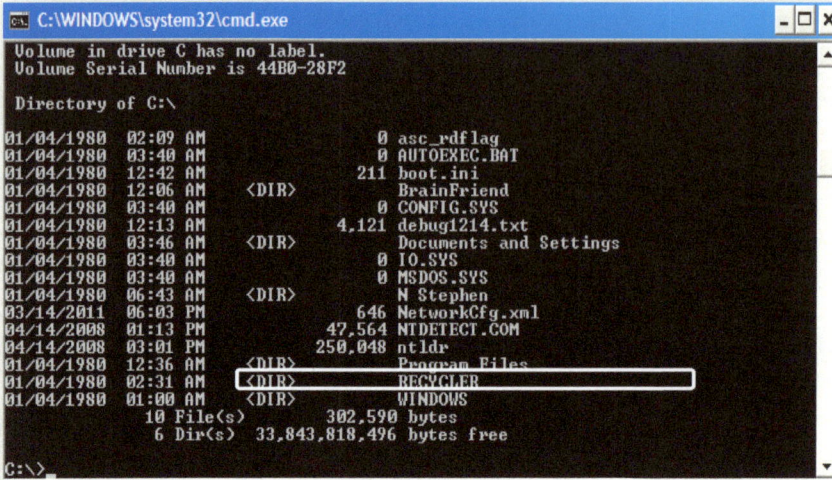

4. The next action is to remove or delete the virus with this command:

del recycler

The computer will reply: c:\recycler*, Are you sure (Y/N)?

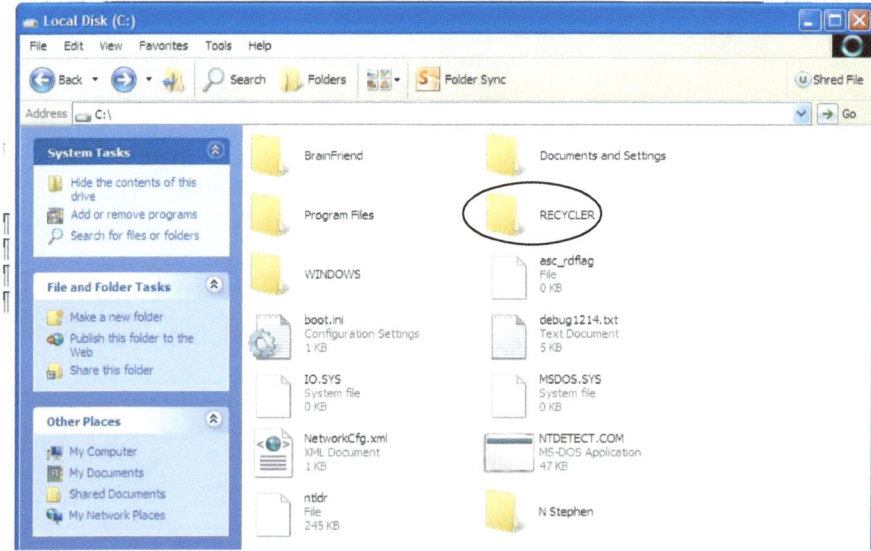

Then press the **'Y'** key, which signifies **'Yes'** to delete the virus.

5. Now go to your Local Disk (know as Hard disk), double-click to open it, use the **'Cut'** command for a folder named **'Recycler',** and **'Paste'** command to paste it on your screen desktop. Delete the folder from there.

6. Exit from the command prompt, and restart the computer.

Note:

If the Recycler has an associate virus, the command "**del recycler**" will not be able to delete it, both in the Local Disk. In this manner, we must apply the below command lines prior to (i.e. before) step 4.

cd recycler

The computer will reply: C:\>RECYCLER>

dir

For example, the computer will reply: C:\>RECYCLER>S-2309-456-09...
Understand that *S-2309-456-09...*may be the name of the associate virus.

While the command prompt remains

C:\>RECYCLER>

Delete the **"associate virus"** and the **carrier folder** with these command lines

del associate-virus-name
for example, del S-2309-456-09...

del infected-folder-name
for example, del recycler

Then proceed to the step 4.

End of Chapter Three
Key Terminologies and Meaning

Terms	Meaning
Anti-Malware	It is a program created specifically to prevent and remove malware from computer, for example, IObit Malware Fighter.
Anti-Virus	It is a program created specifically to prevent and remove virus from computer, for example, AVAST Anti-Virus.
Emulator	A piece of hardware or software that permits a computer system to run programs and process data designed for a different type of computer system.
Malware	A short form of Malicious Software.
Syntax line	It is a command line that represents the order in which a command must be type together with any parameters and switches that follow it, in command prompt application.
Virus	It is a program created specifically to invade into computers and networks with an aim to create havoc on them.

INTRODUCTION

To gain perfect information concerning the quality of computer is not actually accessible when it comes to the point of buying it. This is because the finished-manufacturers normally packaged the systems (computers), although with the guidance and product description manuals, they tried to identify some sufficient information about them, and as well visibly displayed the basic assessing information of them on a particular body of the system. However, dealers in many occasions do not make the computer available to the state that the buyers can have a perfect view of the system information. So the only way to assess the quality is to observe the visibly displayed labeled (external) information. Meanwhile, there are many undisclosed information (system information) as the computer is not powered on. In this condition, the external information labeled by the finished-manufacturers are the disclosed information, while there are internal information serving also as system information, and as well use for analysis on how to rate the quality of computers, but they are not been displayed outwardly.

So in this Chapter, we briefly discussed the external and internal information that can enable an end-user access and as well know the quality of computer during purchasing or after purchased. Though, without normative support, we will not conclude the best computer product, brand or model, rather, an end-user should make a choice based on the brand or model, which will emanate from the necessary factors we will discuss in the chapter.

ANALYZING THE EXTERNAL INFORMATION

At the looks of a computer pack, or purchased, there are external labeled information, which are externally placed just to inform the end-users about the quality of the computer in question. They are mostly information concerned with system brand, model, type of processor, display resolution size, processing speed rate, RAM Size, hard disk storage size, types of operating system (OS), and optional devices like Webcam, Wireless and, Bluetooth, which are operational support devices.

System Brand: By system brand, we are referring to manufacturer of products. In other words, it is a name, usually a trademark of a product, manufacturer, or the product identification name. So Computers are been produced by different finished-manufacturers with different brand names. For instance, we have HP, Acer, Toshiba, Dell, Compaq, and others. They all produced different brands of computers with different names.

Although, for *Evaluation of PC Quality (***EPCQ***)*, we cannot specifically mention that this particular brand of a computer is the best among others, rather we emphasized that end-users should demand for computers, whose maintenance hardware have market supply availability.

System Model: By system model, we are referring to a specific version among different products or products of a specific producer or manufacturer. For example, a particular computer model of Acer Company. Taking computer manufacturing as an example, Acer known as a computer manufacturing company has different computers such as netbook, notebook, laptop, and others, which exist in different models. Take for example, their **eMachine** computer brand with a model name of **eM350**, and model number of **NAV51**.

For **EPCQ** analysis, model as a yardstick is not the ultimate point when making choice of a better computer, rather in a whole; it depicts the type of computer that an end-user is about to purchase or a finished-manufacturer's product. One who has a perfect knowledge of a particular computer product can use its model number to describe the quality of the computer or identify a particular computer. For judgment, we cannot recommend that this particular model among the products of a particular company, say Company X is the best, or this particular model of Company X is better than this particular model of Company Y. This is because each product model has advantages and disadvantages over each other. In addition, what Mr. Zay preferred in *model x* may not be that of Mr. Yay in the same *model x*. Take for instance, in reference to our Acer netbook computers, model NX.RZFAA.018 of Aspire V3-551-8442 has a higher hard disk storage capacity of 750GB when compare to model NX.RZGAA.028 of Aspire V3-571-6475, which has 500GB hard disk storage capacity, but this does not make it to be much better.

Operating System (OS): Early computers of 1980s were of IBM Disk Operating System (IBM DOS) built-in, but today, we have Windows OS, Mac OS, and others. The Windows OS has taking dominance and are of many types such as Windows 2000, Windows XP, Windows Vista, windows 7, Windows 8, et cetera.

For **EPCQ**, many end-users have expressed their views, which indicate that Windows XP is more friendly-using than Windows Vista. In the other hand, some said, Vista is more protective than XP, but these are personal observations as each of them has advantages and disadvantages. But in all, as of when this book was written, many end-users preferred *Windows 7*, which have better features compare to its predecessors. Though, there is an existence of Windows 8, which is higher, but not first-timer-user friendly.

Processor: Like we learnt previously, the speed at which a processor processes information internally is measured in Hertz (Hz). Whereby some processor will be processing in Megahertz (MHz), some are Gigahertz (GHz), and a GHz is equals to 1000MHz, therefore, the higher the GHz or MHz of computer processor, the higher the processing speed of that computer, vice-versa.

Now, from the chronological inventions of processors as we also expressed in CAplus-1 and 2 books, the early processors have lower grade compare to the newer ones. For instance, the *Intel* family is of lower grade value compare to other families. This is also the same to the Pentium and Celeron, Celeron and Dual Core, i.e. according to their chronological inventions. But of the fact is that the major determinant of the quality of any processor is the processing speed rate. For instance, a Celeron processor with 2.20GHz is preferable to that of I.67GHz, and the same to other families. So those whose preference is underlined in hertz should go for computer with a high processing speed rate, but such computer may lack some other qualities.

Moreover, below is a table depicting some common processors with their grading values:

Processor	Family		Processor Grading
	Type	**Family Grading/Rating**	
Intel	80286	3	**4**
	80386	2	
	80486	1	
Pentium	1	6	**3**
	2	5	
	3	4	
	4	3	
	E	2	
	M	1	
Celeron	Has many types and family grades		**2**
Dual Core	Has many types and family grades		**1**
Xeon	Has many types and family grades		**NG**
Atom	Has many types and family grades		**NG**

Notes:
- Not all the processors are listed, but the common ones, except some Intel® Atom.
- The grading is based on numerical term were 1 is preferable to 2, 2 to 3,…n_1 to n_2.
- NG = Not Graded

RAM Size: As we have already learnt, the Random Access Memory (RAM) is a form of computer data storage device, attached indirectly or directly from the CPU to the motherboard. The determinant of the RAM of Computer is its size. For instance a 2.00GB RAM size is preferable to that of 1.00GB, while a 4.00GB is better than that of 2.00GB.

Display Resolution Size: The displaying resolution of a computer is the number of distinct pixels in each dimension, which the computer has the capability to display when outputting data. A pixel is the smallest element used to form the composition of an image on a computer. It is measured in dimension known as pixel dimension (e.g. 1280x768). The computer monitors displayed images by drawing thousands of very small pixels arranged in columns

For output displays, the displaying resolution of a computer depends on the monitor supports in terms of pixels. So the higher the number of the pixels, the better the *displaying resolution*, the higher the display resolution, the more clarity pictures and data that the screen can displays, relatively to the RGB final colour's spectrum.

As we learnt early, the first colour display was **CGA** (Colour Graphics Adapter) developed in 1981, which had a low displaying resolution of (640x200 pixels). This was followed by the HGC (Higher Colour Graphic) in 1982 with a resolution of 720×348 pixels, the **PGA** (Professional Graphic Adapter) in 1984 with a resolution power of 640×480, the **EGA** (Enhanced Graphics Adapter) featuring 640x350 pixels, and others as of that time.

Today, the **VGA**, **XGA** and **SVGA** are common standards. VGA (Video Graphics Array) has 640x480 pixels, SVGA (Super VGA) offers 800x600 pixels, XGA (eXtended Graphics Array) offers (1024x768), and it is by far with a superior clarity. In addition, some netbook computers have 1024x768 pixels, 1024x600 pixels. For **EPCQ**, a displaying size of 1024x768 pixels is better than that of 1024x600 pixels, the same to 800x600 to 640x480

Hard Disk (HDD) Capacity: As we discussed early, a hard disk is an internal storage component that keeps data inside the computer for later use and remains persistent even when the computer has no power. As a storage device, it has a storage capacity or volume just like other storage devices, and the amount of data that a computer can store are determine by the volume. Therefore, by function, the lower the volume, the lower the storage capacity of the relative computer, vice-versa.

Presently, most computers came with hard disk capacity of 60 Gigabyte (GB), 80GB, 160GB, 250GB, even 500GB. For **EPCQ** relatively to storage purpose, where the End-User preference of choice is on storage capacity, computers with high volumes are recommended because they have higher storage capacity.

Optional Devices: Although, not a major yardstick, but to an extent. Optional devices like Webcam, Wireless and, Bluetooth are of choice, when it comes to their uses in a computer. Primarily, the webcam is built for outside shot-taking of picture, whereby it is used for picture snapping and video recording. The wireless device is for internet wireless connection, while Bluetooth enables a wireless transfer or sharing of data such as video, picture, sound, and text from the sourced (sending) computer to the targeted (receiving) device, such as mobile phones or other computers. But, in terms of **EPCQ**, optional devices are of choice because not all computers can have them as components, therefore their recommendation is of objective.

ANALYZING THE INTERNAL INFORMATION

At the operation of a computer, an end-user has access to view the internal information of the available computer, although, most of the information are already labeled externally on the pack, but, they are not sufficient for absolute detail. So viewing the information required some computer advance user techniques via the computer's *Control Panel* exploration, and/or with a third party utility software like ***Advance System Care (ASC)*** software.

The Control Panel View (A case of Windows OS): This displays the overall information setting of a computer, including all the information about the computer. Through it, (the control panel), an end-user can access the basic information of a computer, which are information concerning the computer's windows edition, few system items, computer name, domain, and workgroup settings, the windows activation status, and other information of the computer.

The computer's window edition displays the edition of the *Windows OS* that is running the computer, system information such as system rating, processor, RAM, system type, computer name, fullname, description, and workgroup settings. Take for example, below is a diagram depicting the basic view information of a computer with a product name *eMachine 350; model number of NAV51*. The computer's name is nwankwostephen which is the owner's name.

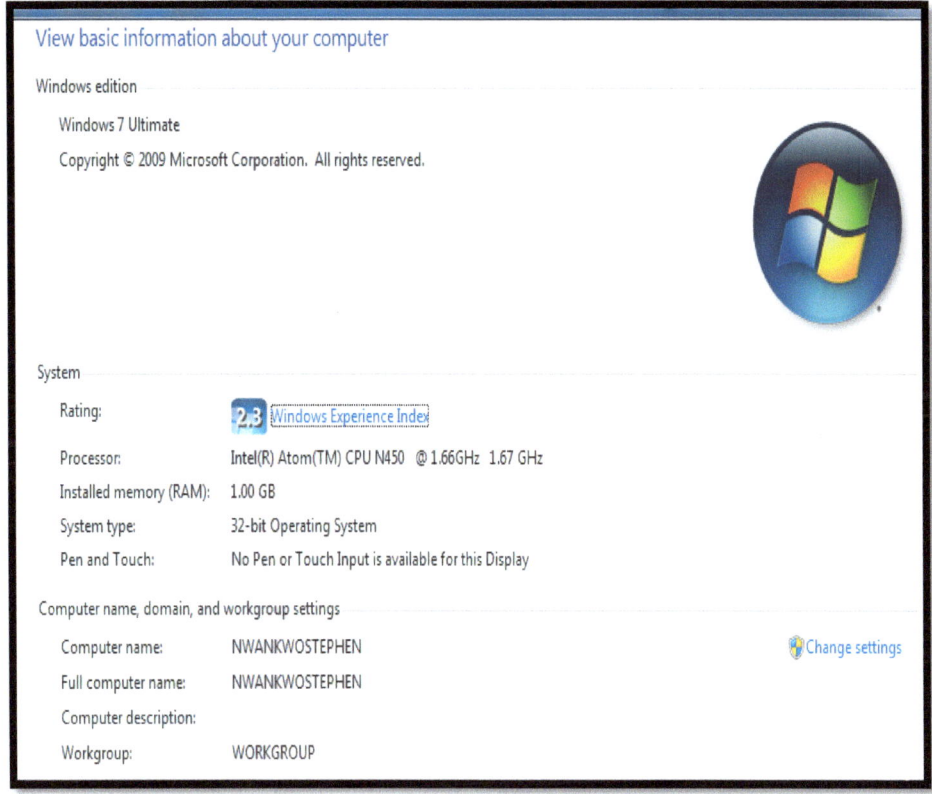

Windows is activated

Product ID: 00426-OEM-8992662-00400

From the diagram above, the computer basic information are classified into four sections, which are the *windows edition section, system, computer name…, and windows activation status.* For its analysis, the *Windows Edition Section* information shows that operating system (OS) of the computer is *Windows 7 Ultimate,* with copyright of Microsoft Corporation. However, there are other Windows 7 versions, such as windows 7 Professional x32, and others, which other computers can have as their OS. In addition is Windows 8, which is preferable.

On the *System Information Section,* the displayed rating of 2.3 *Windows Experience Index* shows that the computer performances and tools rating is *2.3 base score,* which is below when compared to ratings that range from 2.4 to 7.9. We will treat about this later.

The processor type is *Intel*(R) *Atom* with a processing speed rate of 1.66GB. A computer with higher processing speed rate of 2.00GB is preferable. The installed RAM, which is 1.00GB size, is not better than that of 2.00GB, while the system type, which is binary CPU of 32-bit OS, is not better than that of binary CPU of 64-bit OS.

Furthermore, the *Computer Name, Domain and Workgroup Settings* described the computer name, which is *nwankwostephen* or nwankwo Stephen (the owner's name). Finally, the *Windows Activation Status,* which indicates that the running OS of the computer is activated with a *Product ID(identity) of; 00426-OEM-8992662-00400,* therefore indicating that the Windows OS of the computer is not running on trial version status.

PERFORMANCE INFORMATION AND TOOLS RATING

The WEI (*Windows Experience Index*) rating of our depicted computer is *2.3 base score* as been displayed in our diagram. This indicates the performance and overall capability of the computer's hardware. As we mentioned early, 2.3 base score signifies less performance and overall capability of the computer's hardware when compare to results that range from 2.4 to 7.9. For interpretation, this signifies that a result ranges from 2.4 to 7.9 is better off.

What is WEI Rating?

The WEI measures the capability of computer's hardware and software configuration and expresses this measurement as a number called base score. Take for example, a higher base score of 3.1 of Computer X signifies that Computer X will perform better and faster than any computer with a lower base score (for example, 2.7), especially when performing more advanced and resource-intensive tasks.

How does the rating analysis is been access? Each hardware component in the computer will receive individual sub-score, and then the computer's base score will be determined by the lowest sub-score. For example, if the lowest sub-score of a particular individual hardware component is 2.6, then the base score of the accessing computer will be 2.6. However, the base score is not an average of the combined sub-scores, but it can give an end-user a view of how the components that are most important to the computer will perform, and can help decide which components to upgrade.

The Important of Base Score

The primary benefit of the base score is that it can serve as notification for programs and other software purchases. End-users can use it (base score) to make decision when there is a need to buy programs and other software that are compatible to their computer's base score. For example, if a computer has a base score of 3.3, then a user can buy any software designed for this version of Windows that requires a computer with a base score of 3.0 or lower. The scores currently scale from 1.0 minimum to 7.9 maximum. Moreover, below are the general descriptions of the experience an end-user can expect from Windows 7 computers that receives the following base scores:

- A computer with a base score of 1.0 or 2.0 usually has sufficient performance to do with general computing tasks, such as running office productivity programs and searching of the Internet. Although, not powerful enough to run Aero, or the advanced multimedia experiences that are available with Windows 7 OS.

- A computer with a base score of 3.0 can run Aero and many features of Windows 7 at a basic level. Some of the Windows 7 advanced features might not have all of their functionality available. For example, a computer with a base score of 3.0 can display the Windows 7 theme at a resolution of 1280 × 1024, but might struggle to run the theme on multiple monitors. Or, it can play digital TV content but might struggle to play high-definition television (HDTV) content.

- A computer with a base score of 4.0 or 5.0 can run new features of Windows 7, and it can support running multiple programs at the same time.

- A computer with a base score of 6.0 or 7.0 has a faster hard disk, and can support high-end, graphics-intensive experiences, such as multiplayer and 3-D gaming, recording and playback of HDTV content.

Furthermore, if a particular program or Windows OS observation requires a higher score than an existing base score, the end-user can upgrade the hardware in order to meet the necessary base score. If, for instance, you installed new hardware, and want to see if your score has changed, click *Re-run the assessment*. However, if you are prompted for an administrator password or confirmation, type the password or provide confirmation. To view details about the hardware on your computer, *click View and print details*.

The diagram below displays the rate and improved-performances of our sample computer, which is *nwankwostephen*. It shows that the computer base score is 2.3.

Component	What is rated	Subscore	Base score
Processor:	Calculations per second	2.3	
Memory (RAM):	Memory operations per second	4.5	
Graphics:	Desktop performance for Windows Aero	2.8	**2.3**
Gaming graphics:	3D business and gaming graphics performance	3.0	Determined by lowest subscore
Primary hard disk:	Disk data transfer rate	5.3	

Rate and improve your computer's performance

The Windows Experience Index assesses key system components on a scale of 1.0 to 7.9.

EPCQ BASED ON UTILITY SOFTWARE (A CASE OF ASC VER. 3.7.2 SOFTWARE)

Like we learned in system software analyses of CAplus-1 book, utility software or programs are system software (mostly third party software) designed to help computer for proper system performances. They are mostly referred as software and hardware computer tools. For instance, every installed Windows OS comes along with these utility tools, however, computer end-users can as well through websites; download a third party utility tool that will be suitable for computers. In this case, *Advance System Care (ASC), version 3.7.2* is one of them. Following a proper technical use of the software (ASC ver. 3.7.2) on our sample computer, named; *nwankwostephen*, we got the below diagrams bearing the system information (i.e. the computer information) of *nwankwostephen*. The utility software classified the system information into some categories such as, *operating system, processor and motherboard, memory device, drives, display, network,* and *other devices.*

For simplification, and in conjunction with brief highlights, we presented the shotsnaps of the diagrams as they represented each set of the system information. Although, most of the information are for advance analysis, so we did not go into full details, and each of the diagram is in default division of two table columns named; *the item name column* and *value column.* In addition, any item name bearing *"status"* with respective of value of *"ok"* signifies that, that particular device is working properly. Below are the diagrams with explanations.

1) The Operating System Information Diagram

From the diagram below, the operating system information just like the rest of other diagrams, is divided into two table columns named; *the item name column* and *value column.* The main system information, which are displayed on *the item name column* are the computer system, operating system and registry information, and each of them has its sub-categorized information with their various respective values. But, for awareness, the registry is a database in Windows that contains important information about system hardware, installed programs and settings, and profiles of each of the user accounts on a computer. It is mandated that windows continually refers to the information in the registry.

Item Name	Value
Computer System	
Computer Name	NWANKWOSTEPHEN
User Name	NWANKWO STEPHEN
Organization	
Operating System	
OS Name	Microsoft Windows 7 Ultimate
OS Version	6.1.7600
Product ID	00426-OEM-8992662-00400
System Uptime	12/11/2010 11:07:57 PM
Internet Explorer Version	8.0.7600.16385
Microsoft DirectX Version	10.0
OpenGL Version	6.1.7600.16385 (win7_rtm.090713-1255)
Free Physical Memory	115 MB
Free Page File	950 MB
Free Virtual Memory	1065 MB
Registry	
Maximum Size	682MB
Current Size	58MB
Status	OK

2) **The Processor and Motherboard Information Diagram**

From the diagram, the main system information displayed on the *item name column* are the central processor, motherboard and BIOS information, and each of them has its respective values displayed on the value column side of the table.

Item Name	Value
☐ ❖ Center Processor	
CPU Name	Intel(R) Atom(TM) CPU N450 @ 1.66GHz
Code Name	
Manufacturer	GenuineIntel
Current Clock Speed	1666Mhz
Max Clock Speed	1666Mhz
Voltage	1.6V
External Clock	667Mhz
Serial Number	BFE9FBFF000106CA
CPU ID	x64 Family 6 Model 28 Stepping 10
Socket Designation	CPU
Unknown	512KB
Unknown	32KB
☐ 🖳 Motherboard	
Model	eM350
Manufacturer	Acer
Serial Number	Base Board Serial Number
BIOS Name	InsydeH2O Version V1.03
BIOS Vendor	Acer
SMBIOS Version	V1.03
BIOS Date	5/27/2010
☐ 🔲 BIOS Features	
PCI is supported	Yes
BIOS is Upgradable (Flash)	Yes
BIOS shadowing is allowed	Yes
Boot from CD is supported	Yes
Selectable Boot is supported	Yes

3) **The Memory Device Information Diagram**

From the diagram, the main system information displayed on the *item name* column are the memory resource and physical memory information of the computer, and each of them has its respective values displayed on the value column side of the table.

Item Name	Value
⊟ ⓘ Memory Resource	
Total Memory	1013 MB
Used Memory	862 MB
Free Memory	150 MB
Memory Usage	85%
⊟ 🔲 Physical Memory	
Memory Bank	BANK 0
Description	Physical Memory 0
Device Location	DIMM0
Capacity	1024 MB
Speed	667Mhz
Manufacturer	Kinston
Data Width	64bit
Memory Type	
Form Factor	SODIMM

4) <u>The Disk Drive Information Diagram</u>

From the diagram, the main system information displayed on the item name column are the disk drive and Integrated Device Electronics (IDE) controllers information of the computer, and each of them has its respective values displayed on the value column side of the table.

Item Name	Value
⊟ 🖴 Disk drive	
Name	Hitachi HTS545016B9A300 ATA Device
Media Type	Fixed hard disk media
Capacity	160GB
Interface Type	IDE
Partitions	3
Total Cylinders	19457
Total Heads	255
Total Sectors	312576705
Total Tracks	4961535
Tracks Per Cylinder	255
Sectors Per Track	512
Bytes Per Sector	63
S.M.A.R.T Support	Yes
Current Temperature	41C (105.8F)
⊟ 🖴 IDE Controller	
Name	ATA Channel 0
Manufacturer	(Standard IDE ATA/ATAPI controllers)
Status	OK
⊟ 🖴 IDE Controller	
Name	ATA Channel 1
Manufacturer	(Standard IDE ATA/ATAPI controllers)
Status	OK
⊟ 🖴 IDE Controller	
Name	Standard AHCI 1.0 Serial ATA Controller
Manufacturer	Standard AHCI 1.0 Serial ATA Controller
Status	OK

5) The Display Information Diagram

From the diagram, the main system information displayed on the item name column are the video adapter and monitor information of the computer, and each of them has its respective values displayed on the value column side of the table.

Item Name	Value
☐ 🖳 Video Adapter	
Name	Intel(R) Graphics Media Accelerator 3150
Video Processor	Intel(R) Graphics Media Accelerator 3150
Manufacturer	Intel Corporation
Video Architecture	VGA
DAC Type	Internal
Memory Size	256MB
Memory Type	Unknown
Video Mode	1024 x 600 x 4294967296 colors
Current Refresh Rate	59Hz
Driver Version	8.14.10.2117
Driver Date	4/19/2010
☐ 🖥 Monitor	
Name	Generic PnP Monitor
Screen Height	600
Screen Width	1024
Status	OK

6) The Network Information Diagram

From the diagram, the main system information displayed on the item name column are the Local Area Connection (for LAN) and Wireless Network Connection (WAN) information of the computer, and each of them has its respective values displayed on the value column side of the table.

Item Name	Value
Local Area Connection	
Product Name	Atheros AR8132 PCI-E Fast Ethernet Controller (NDIS 6.20)
Driver File	L1C
Manufacturer	Atheros
MAC Address	88:AE:1D:19:AA:BD
Wireless Network Connection	
Product Name	Atheros AR5B95 Wireless Network Adapter
Driver File	athr
Manufacturer	Atheros Communications Inc.
MAC Address	C4:46:19:1C:8D:51

7) **The Other Device Information Diagram**

From the diagram, the main system information displayed on the item name column are the sound, keyboard, USB Controllers information of the computer, and each of them has its respective values displayed on the value column side of the table.

Item Name	Value
Sound Device	
Name	High Definition Audio Device
Manufacturer	Microsoft
Status	OK
Keyboard	
Name	Launch Manager
Description	Enhanced (101- or 102-key)
Function Keys	12
Status	OK
USBController	
Product Name	Intel(R) N10/ICH7 Family USB Universal Host Controller - 27C8
Manufacturer	Intel
Protocol Supported	Universal Serial Bus
Status	OK
USBController	
Product Name	Intel(R) N10/ICH7 Family USB Universal Host Controller - 27C9
Manufacturer	Intel
Protocol Supported	Universal Serial Bus
Status	OK
USBController	
Product Name	Intel(R) N10/ICH7 Family USB Universal Host Controller - 27CA
Manufacturer	Intel
Protocol Supported	Universal Serial Bus
Status	OK
USBController	

Command Prompt Display of System Information

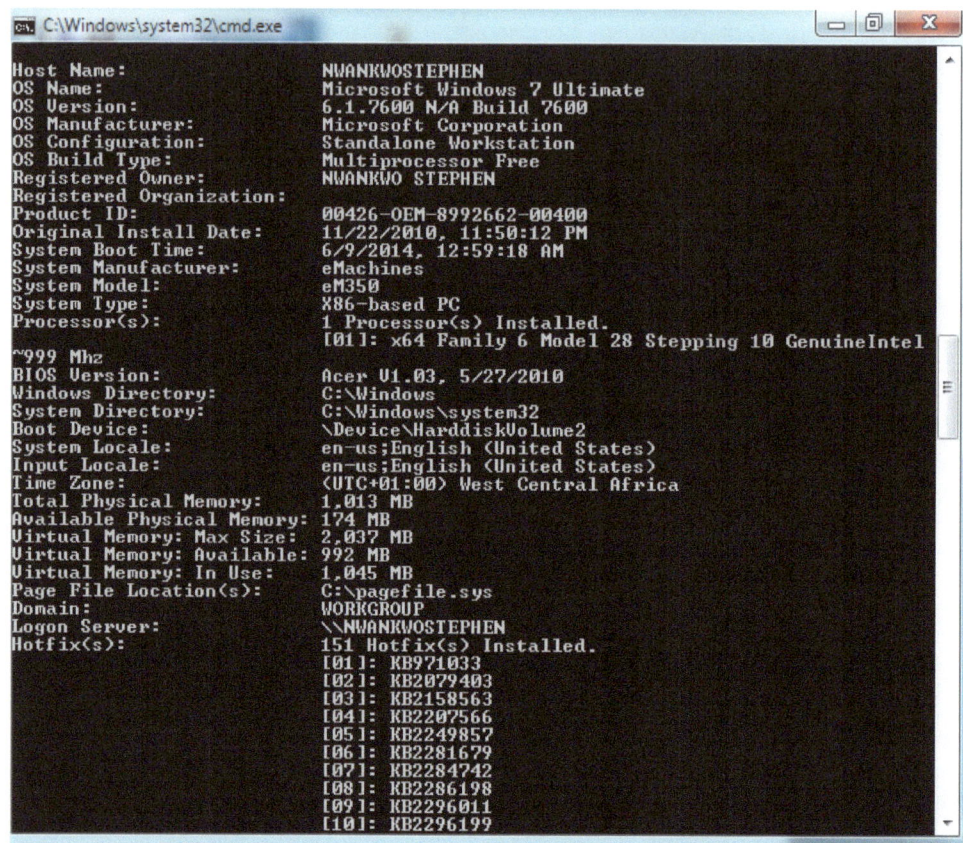

A scroll down part of the first display

EPCQ Conclusion for Windows Computer

From our evaluating processes so far, we cannot conclude that this particular computer's brand name or model is the best, rather we can classify the qualities based on Normal, Good, and Better Quality in relation to few components.

Components	Normal Quality	Good Quality	Better Quality
System Brand	nn	nn	nn
System Model	nn	nn	nn
System type by Integer Representative	32-bit OS	64-bit OS	64-bit OS
Operating System type	Vista or Windows XP	Windows 7	Windows 8
RAM Size	= or >1G	= or >2G	= or >4G
Speed of Processor	= or > 1GHz	= or > 2GHz	= or > 4GHz
Processor	Intel/Pentium Family	Celeron Family	Dual Core family
Hard disk Size	= or >160GB	= or > 250GB	= or >500GB
Monitor	CRT	TFT-LCD or PDP	
Optional Devices	Webcam	Wireless, and Webcam	Wireless, Bluetooth, and Webcam
WEI Rating	= or > 2.5	= or > 3.0	= or > 4.0
Battery Type	NiMH, NiCad, etc.	Normal Lithium-ion	An upgraded Lithium-ion
Hardware Marketing Availability	Few	Moderate	Everywhere

Notes

1. For learning more about System type by Integer Representative, read the topic of "Components of CPU" in CAplus-2 book.

2. nn = not necessary.

3. Hardware Marketing Availability should be determined base on Company name. E.g. Acer, HP, etc.

4. Display Resolution Size can be determined based on Screen size.

5. CRT = Cathode Ray Tube

6. TFT-LCD = Thin-film Transistor-Liquid Crystal Display

7. PDP = Plasma Display Panel

End of Chapter Four

Key Terminologies and Meaning

Terms	Meaning
Display Resolution Size	The display resolution of a computer is the number of distinct pixels in each dimension, which the computer has the capability to display.
Integer Representative	It is the size and precision of numbers of location or address that CPU can represent in computer. In other words, it is the number of location in computer memory that CPU can address when carrying out its function, such as logical or arithmetic functions.
LAN	It stands for Local Area Network.
	It stands for Wireless Area Network.
Model	This is a specific version among different products or articles of a specific producer or manufacturer, for example, system model of a particular computer model of Acer Company.
System Brand	This is a name, usually a trademark of a product or manufacturer, or the product identification name, let say Acer computer.
WEI Rating	The WEI measures the capability of a computer's hardware and software configuration and expresses this measurement as a number called a base score.

Objectives Assessment of Chapter Three

1. Examine yourself whether you perfectly achieved the objectives of this last lesson, if not, read it again. However, if you have any question regarding to what you have learnt, visit www.onlineworkdata.com.

2. If you are successful, move to the **Practical Activities.**

Practical Activities of the Book

1.) Practical Activity

You are to open a Gmail account.

    1. Connect to Internet, and Click your web browser

    2. On the "address bar of the web browser, type 'gmail.com'

    4. Click "Create an Account"

    5. Fill the Form with your personal data and submit it.

    6. Please make sure your phone can receive call.

You are to open a Facebook account, and Join us at Facebook.

Assuming you already on Internet:

    1. Click your web browser

    2. On the "address bar of the web browser, type "facebook.com"

    3. Fill the Form and Click "Sign Up"

    4. Continue until, the final stage and submit it.

    5. Please make sure your phone can receive SMS.

You are Join us at Facebook.

To join us at Facebook, you can search us in your "Login In" Facebook web page. **On search "friends bar"**, type "Speds", and add as a friend.

Alternatively,

Assuming you already on Internet

    1. Click your web browser

    2. On the "address bar of the web browser, type **"www.onlineworkdata.com"**

    3. Click our Facebook place on the "Home" page

    4. As the Facebook page open, enter your Facebook email address, and submit it.

2.) Practical Activity

You are to find out the basic quality of a computer

1. Get a laptop and place it on a table;

2. Without switching on the laptop, look on the edge (top) of the keyboard, and identify the followings:

   - The processor type of the computer
   - The RAM size,
   - The Hard disk size
   - Look straight on the screen of the laptop, check if you will see a camera lens, indicating that the laptop has a webcam
   - Check on the F-keys of the keyboard, if you find a key with an antenna symbol, know that the laptop has Wi-Fi,

3. Switch on the computer and examine the quality of the internal components. This has to be done in the Control Panel of the Computer. To access the Control Panel,

   i. Click the Start button
   ii. Inside the pop window of the Start menu, look for the Control Panel, but if you cannot find it, click All-Programs,
   iii. From the All-Programs, click Accessories > System tools > Control Panel

Now you have opened the Control Panel,

1. Click System and Security > System

2. Examine the Control Panel view to notice the Base Score Rating, Processor Type and Speed Rate, RAM Size, System Type, etc. See sample below:

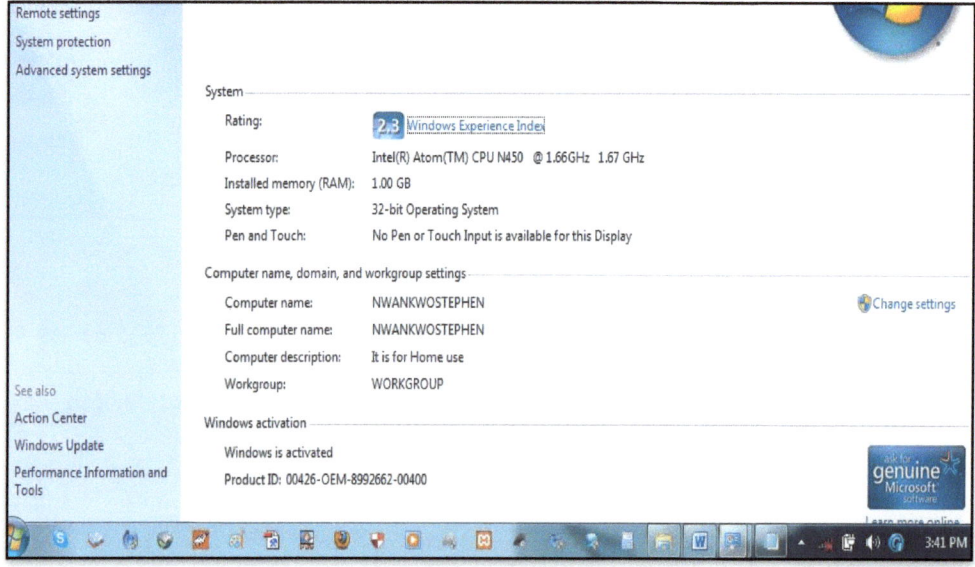

3.) Practical Activity

If you are a city dweller, and have access to any Desktop Computer or PC, learn about the followings:

1. How to setup a desktop computer, given the availability of a monitor, keyboard, system unit, mouse, and all the necessary chords.

2. Access All-Programs and System Tools by clicking the Starts button.

3. Learn about anti-virus through **www.google.com**, search engine.

4. Review the technical skills of:

   i. How to Prevent Threats
   ii. How to Remove Threats
   iii. How to Publish documents both in XPS and PDF

4.) Practical Activity

Objectives Assessment of the Book

1. Examine yourself whether you perfectly achieved the objectives of this book, if not, read it again. However, if you have any question regarding to what you have learnt, visit **www.onlineworkdata.com**.

2. If you are successful, move the book to your **Library.**

3. See the last page of this book for other helpful books.

5.) Practical Activity

Using of Word Count in Microsoft Windows 2007 and 2010.

1. Click and open Microsoft Word Program, via the Desktop or Start button,
2. The text below, copy or type it inside the document of the MS Word,

> *CAplus books are in four packs of CAplus-1, 2, 3, and 4.*
> *I will like to have all of them.*

For example, see the below picture.

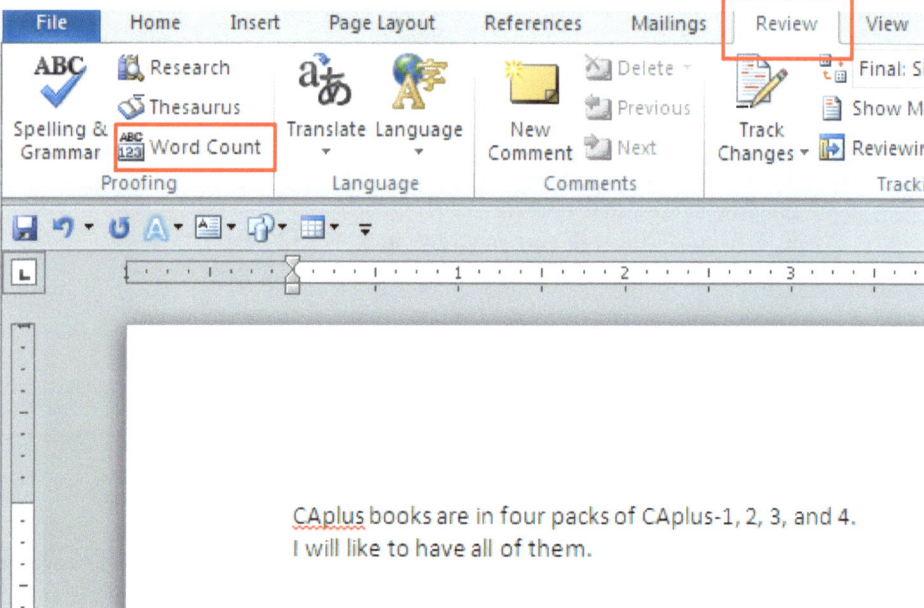

3. At the Ribbon bar of the Application, click the **Review** ribbon,

4. On the **Proofing** tab, click the **Word Count** tool, and view the below window:

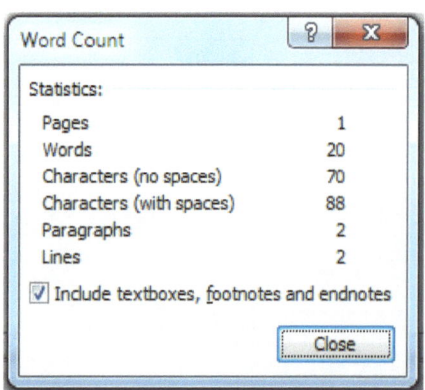

Using the
Characters (with space),
which is 88, the total byte of
the text is 11B.

REFERENCES

Cybercrime, (2011). **Encyclopedia Britannica, Ultimate Reference Suite.** Chicago: Encyclopedia Britannica.

Engber, Daniel (Jan. 17, 2014). "Who Made That CAPTCHA". Nytimes.com. NYT. Retrieved January.17, 2014.

N. Stephen (2014), **CAplus-1.** Space-Era Data Services, www.onlineworkdata.com

Walsh, Eric (Oct. 28, 2013). **"CAPTCHA he cracked by artificial intelligence"**. mybroadband.co.za. Reuters. Retrieved. Nov. 27 2013

Windows 7 Ultimate (2009): **Windows Help and Support files**. Microsoft Corporation.

Supported websites:

http://compgeekss.blogspot.com/2009/01/removing-autoruninf-virus-viruses-that.html

http://en.wikipedia.org/wiki/Creeper_virus

http://en.wikipedia.org/wiki/Lahore,_Pakistan

http://en.wikipedia.org/wiki/Talk:Computer_virus

http://home.web.cern.ch/topics/birth-web

http://walthowe.com/navnet/history.html

www.studymode.com/essays/history-of-computer-virus-330922.html

Note:

1. I made a tremendous search by going through the materials, when writing this book, please understand that information posted on a website is subject for updates and removal, and therefore take note as this may affect your reference search.

INDEX

A

Actual Activities 47
Address Bar 7, 53, 54, 107
Adware 65, 66, 68
Anti-malware 79, 81, 82, 88
Anti-virus 69, 72, 73, 77, 82, 88
Application Software 2, 8, 28, 43
Autorun Infection 72, 84

B

Battery Types 105
Bit 33
Blogger 48, 63, 72
Bluetooth 92, 105
Bots 62, 63
Browser Configuration 77
Byte 33

C

CAPTCHA 62
Ccleaner 78
Celeron 91, 105
CERN 46
Character 33
Command Prompt 15, 24, 27
Common Features of Windows 7
Compose Email 56, 58, 63
Computer Threat 65
Control Panel 25, 26
CRT 105

D

DARPA 46
Data 33
Default Folders 17, 20
Desktop Computer 4
Desktop Environment 3, 7, 10
Dialog Box 11
Disk Operating System 23, 73, 90
Display Control Buttons 7
Display Resolution Size 90, 92, 106
Domain Name 53
Draft Box 56, 63
Drive 17, 19, 70, 72
Dual-Core 91, 95
DVI Port 4, 5

E

E-Learning 47, 51
Email 2
Email Client 28
Email Service Providers 53, 56
Emulator 71, 88
Extranet 46

F

File Extension 35, 37, 43, 74
File-naming 34
Folder 15
Forum 50, 56
FTP 43

G

Gigabyte 33, 92
Gigahertz 91
Graphical User Interface 7, 25, 43
Graphic Hardware 3, 7

H

Hackers 53, 66, 69, 75, 76
Hard Disk 12, 15, 19
Hard Disk Capacity 92
Hecto-byte 33
HDTV 95
Http 53

I

Icon 16
Inbox 56
Information 33
Integer Representative 105, 106
INTEL 91
Intel Atom 91
Internet Protocol (IP) 43
Intranet 45, 46
IObit Malware Fighter 79, 81, 82
IP Address 63

K

Kilobyte 33

L

LAN 106
Linux 3
Local Disk 17, 19, 20

M

Main Hardware 4
Malware 2, 65, 66
Mac OS 3
Megabyte 33
Megahertz 91
Microsoft Office 28
Model 90, 93
MODEM 55
Mozilla Firefox 54, 77
Menu Bar 7

N

Network 46
Notification-area 13, 14

O

Offline Prevention 75, 80, 81
Online Prevention 75, 76, 81
Outbox 56, 63

P

Peripheral Hardware 4
Password 35, 45, 56, 57
PDF 34, 35
Plasma Display Panel 105
Pentium 91, 105
Power Cables 6
Processor 91, 94, 98
PS/2 4, 6

R

RAM Size 92
Recycle Bin 10, 12
Recycler 70, 84, 85, 86, 87
Ribbon Bar 7, 8
Rootkits 65, 67, 69

S

Scroll Bar 7, 8
Search Engine 46, 49, 62
Sent Box 56, 63
Sign In 56, 63
Sign Out 56, 63
Sign Up 56, 63
Social Networking n50, 56, 63
Spam box 56, 63
Spammers 56, 63
Spyware 65, 66, 67
Start-Button 10, 13, 19
Status Bar 7, 8, 13, 15
Syntax Line 27, 72, 82, 88
System Brand 90, 105, 106
System Model 90, 105, 106
System Tools 23, 24, 43

T

Table Desktop 4, 5
Task Bar 10, 13, 22
Task Manager 14
Terabyte 33
TFT-LCD 105
Title Bar 7, 8
Tool Bar 7, 53
Tower Desktop 4, 5
Trash Box 56, 63
Trash Can 16
Trojan 27, 65, 66

U

URL 45, 53, 54
USB Flash Drive 75, 80
USB Port 4
USB Disk Security 80, 81, 83
Username and Password 57

V

VGA Port 4, 5
Virtual Activities 47
Virus 68

W

WAN 106
Web browser 7, 53
Webcam 90, 92, 95
Webinar 51
Weblog 45, 48, 63
Webpage 53, 56, 63
Webserver 53
Website 46, 47
WEI Rating 94, 105
Wiki 49
Windows 2, 3
Windows Command Processor 27
Windows Firewall 76
Worm 65, 67
WWW 46

X

Xeon 91
XPS 35, 37, 38

Other Available Computer Books

APP-XL PLUS APP-XL SOLUTION PACK 1.0.0

APPLIED MICROSOFT EXCEL IN STATISTICS,
ECONOMICS, BUSINESS, AND FINANCE PERSPECTIVE:
FOR MICROSOFT EXCEL USERS AND LEARNERS

N. STEPHEN

CAPLUS -2

The Hardware and The Software,
for advanced learning.

N. STEPHEN

App-XL Solution Pack 1.0.0

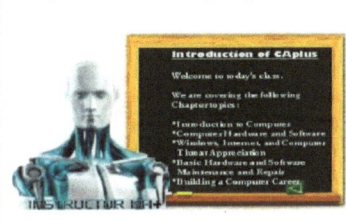

CAPLUS-1

COMPUTER APPRECIATION PLUS,
FOR BASIC AND ADVANCE LEARNING.

N. STEPHEN

www.ingramcontent.com/pod-product-compliance
Lightning Source LLC
Chambersburg PA
CBHW050720180526
45159CB00003B/1088